DOCUMENTS OF MODERN HISTORY

KU-372-860

General Editors:

A. G. Dickens
The Director, Institute of Historical Research, University of London

Alun Davies
Professor of Modern History, University College, Swansea

FROM ISOLATION TO CONTAINMENT, 1921–1952

Three Decades of American Foreign Policy from Harding to Truman

edited by

Richard D. Challener
Professor of History, Princeton University

WITHDRAWN

CHESTER COLLEGE
ACC. No.
71|70
DEPT.
CLASS No.
973.91088327
CHA
LIBRARY

Edward Arnold

© Richard D. Challener 1970

First Published 1970 by
Edward Arnold (Publishers) Ltd.
41 Maddox Street, London W1

Boards Edition SBN : 7131 5478 0
Paper Edition SBN : 7131 5479 9

Acknowledgments

The editor and publishers wish to thank the following for their permission to use copyright material: The Houghton Mifflin Company for documents I (4), pp. 16-17 and III (4), pp. 53-7; The Herbert Hoover Foundation for document IV (2a), pp. 98-103; The McGraw-Hill Book Company for document IV (12), pp. 108-9; William Morrow and Company Inc. and James Brown Associates Inc. for document V (5a), pp. 122-3; The Franklin D. Roosevelt Library for document V (5b), pp. 133-5; The W.C.C. Publishing Company Inc., and Princeton University for documents VI (1), pp. 143-4 and VI (2b), pp. 146-7, and Sullivan and Cromwell for document VI (7), pp. 174-81.

Printed in Great Britain by
R. & R. Clark, Ltd., Edinburgh

CONTENTS

INTRODUCTION

The documents in this volume cover the years from 1921 to 1952, from the administration of Warren Harding to that of Harry Truman. They seek to illustrate the evolution of American foreign policy from isolation to containment and the great change from rejection of international commitments to full-scale involvement in the politics of world power.

There is an underlying unity to a book of this scope. In the twenties the United States, having spurned the Wilsonian programme, was trying to define the role it should play in world affairs, and, as the documents suggest, it played a considerably larger role than conventional historical accounts imply. In the thirties, as a new conflict began to develop, America did turn inwards, tried to isolate itself from the coming storm, and then belatedly, and against all intentions, became involved. But after 1945, during the Truman years, the United States went through what can only be described as a 'revolution' in both its military and foreign policies. Ultimately America became the spearhead of a vast, intricate design to create a new system of international power that would contain the Soviet Union and its allies. It became involved in a far-flung system of peace-time military alliances which bound the United States more firmly than the old alliance systems of 1914 had bound the members of the Triple Entente and the Triple Alliance. By 1949 America was conducting a foreign policy which was precisely the opposite of virtually everything in its diplomatic tradition.

There is good reason to stop at 1952. The main lines of the diplomatic revolution were outlined in a few short years after 1947, and the basic foundation of the cold war policy of the United States was established during the years that Harry Truman occupied the White House. To be sure, there were many vocal critics; at times it appeared as if the revolution would be undone or at least greatly modified. But the Eisenhower administration, however much it lashed out against the 'sterile' policy of containment, actually carried it forward and consolidated it. Dulles and Eisenhower built upon the foundations laid by Truman, Marshall, and Acheson; historians may well remember them more for carrying on what they inherited rather than for their innovations. Moreover, in the process they created a public consensus on matters of foreign policy.

By the 1960s that consensus had begun to disintegrate. President John F. Kennedy yearned to break with the orthodoxies of the Cold War, while men like Senator William Fulbright, pointing to the fact that communism had lost its monolithic character, called upon Americans to discard the 'old myths' and face up to the 'new realities'. By the mid-sixties, especially after the follies and frustrations of Vietnam, the voices of dissent had become loud throughout the land, especially the thunder from the New Left. But the breakdown of the Eisenhower consensus and the rise of radical dissent emerged as a consequence of vast changes within the United States as well as within the Communist world. To attempt a documentary survey of these events and phenomena would be to open an entirely new and vast subject, one that properly requires a volume of its own and which lies well beyond the compass of the present selection.

In order to emphasise key themes and heighten readability, I have heavily edited many of the documents in this volume. For similar reasons I have, wherever possible, relied upon political speeches and memoir material rather than the more formal correspondence of the diplomats. Limitations of space have meant that the selection of documents is less complete than I would ideally have liked; nevertheless I believe that the following pages include a representative sample suggestive of both the scope of and the changes in three decades of American foreign policy.

RICHARD D. CHALLENER

Princeton, N.J.
August 26, 1968

I

THE 1920S: PEACE, DISARMAMENT AND WORLD AFFAIRS

There is a widespread belief that Americans, after rejecting Wilson's vision of a new world order, set out in relentless pursuit of what Warren Harding called 'normalcy' and sought to return to the comfortable refuge of isolationism. The documents in this section have been selected to demonstrate that the so-called 'return to isolation' belongs in large measure to the world of myth and that the Republican administrations of Harding, Coolidge and Hoover did play a not inconsiderable role in world affairs. There are, however, significant qualifications. America usually played its role in the most awkward and back-handed fashion, as if pretending it was not a great power. Moreover, no Republican President or Secretary of State was willing to assume any political commitments in the international area, to consider any proposals for collective security or to accept any limitations upon American freedom of action. Nevertheless, within this restricted context, the United States was involved in a wide spectrum of affairs: economic expansion, German reparations, naval and land disarmament, the creation of a new treaty system for the Far East, many of the non-political endeavours of the League of Nations, and, above all, the peace movement.

The terms of the separate treaty of peace signed with Germany in 1921 suggest the countervailing tendencies: on the one hand, the United States again bluntly asserted its total rejection of the League of Nations, while, on the other, it was careful to reserve for itself 'all the rights, privileges . . . or advantages' of the Versailles Treaty that it refused to ratify (1). There was a similar approach to international economic issues. The United States, having emerged from the war as the world's great creditor nation, was anxious to expand its overseas economic horizons. As a State Department press release clearly indicates, cabinet members as well as bankers expressed great interest in floating foreign loans in the American market. But the administration, wedded to the tenets of free enterprise, only obliquely posed the question of the extent to which such loans involved the national interest or should be subject to any form of government supervision (**2(a)**).

However, the ambivalence of the Republican 'straddle' in foreign policy was most clearly revealed in the handling of German reparations. America, like Britain, believed that the prosperity of Europe depended upon the economic health of Germany and bitterly opposed the French occupation of the Ruhr. Yet, year in and year out, the United States refused to recognise that there was any legal, moral or logical connection between reparations and Allied war debts to America or to agree that the American government should become directly involved in the reparations issue. Hence, when Secretary of State Charles Evans Hughes chose to reveal his own formula for reparations, he addressed his remarks not to the Allied or German governments but to an audience of American academics at their annual professional convention. Hughes, after denying that the Allied war debts figured in the economic equation, outlined a proposal to take reparations 'out of politics' by appointing a special group of financial experts; he added the masterful subterfuge that, if such an assembly of technicians was called together, he was certain that 'distinguished Americans' would be delighted to participate if invited (**2 (b)**). From this roundabout beginning there eventually emerged the Dawes Plan, the first even halfway sensible attempt to grapple with reparations.

Far Eastern questions attracted a great amount of American attention in the early 1920s. It was the United States which sponsored the far-reaching Washington Conference of 1921–22. Behind the conference call was an insistent American demand to halt the burgeoning naval race between Great Britain, Japan and the United States. But America was equally interested in settling a wide range of outstanding Far Eastern political issues – ranging from a hope to end the long distrusted Anglo-Japanese Treaty to a desire to secure international recognition for the 'Open Door' in China. The Washington Conference produced a multitude of treaties: naval disarmament and non-fortification agreements in the Pacific, the Four Power Pact and the Nine Power Pact. Taken together these created a new political order in the Pacific and established the framework within which Far Eastern affairs were to be handled for more than a decade. Secretary Hughes's speech at the opening session of the Washington Conference is one of the most famous addresses in American diplomatic history. It dealt largely with naval disarmament – indeed, called for such drastic cuts in naval power that the *Manchester Guardian* observed that in a few minutes Hughes had sunk more British battleships than all of Europe's admirals in a cycle of centuries. But although the speech touched only fleetingly on the broader political questions of the Far East that were to figure so heavily in the ensuing work of the conference, it well illustrates that the horizons of American foreign policy in the early 1920s still extended into the far Pacific (**3**).

At the outset of the decade the League of Nations was, of course, anathema to the Republicans. The trials and tribulations of Joseph C. Grew, the American minister to Switzerland, belong to the world of Gilbert and Sullivan but clearly indicate how completely the United States rejected the den of internationalists at Geneva (**4 (a)**). However, by the close of the twenties, the attitude had softened, and the United States participated, both formally and informally, in an increasing number of the economic and social endeavours of the League. But it would never involve itself in the political work of the League. When the League attempted to strengthen its machinery for collective security, Hughes's rejection of the abortive Geneva Protocol was prompt, complete and thoroughly in keeping with the American repudiation of the political role of the League (4 (b)).

But Americans, as numerous historians have observed, were always interested in the cause of world peace and ever anxious to find some magic formula which, avoiding both Geneva and 'power politics', would prevent another world war. Never in American history was interest in the peace crusade greater than in the twenties. The culmination of this vast effort was the Kellogg-Briand Pact (Treaty of Paris) of 1928, according to which nations around the world solemnly promised that they would never again resort to war (though they were free to engage in wars of self defence and, indeed, to decide whether or not a particular war qualified as self defence). The Kellogg Pact was, if nothing else, a tribute to the tenacity and strength of the American peace movement, for neither a reluctant Secretary of State, Kellogg, nor a sceptical President Coolidge would have become converts to the cause if they had not been pressured into it by the highly organized peace crusaders and their allies. The Kellogg Pact has since come to symbolize the lack of realism in American foreign policy in the 1920s; yet, though the effort was misguided, even at times pathetically ludicrous, it was a high-water point in the American quest to banish war from the world (5).

It was an effort which did not die with the end of the twenties. One of the last major efforts of the Hoover administration was a far-reaching proposal for the disarmament of land armies which the Quaker President submitted to the Geneva Disarmament Conference of 1932. That conference, sponsored by the League and intended to bring to a head the labours of Geneva for world peace, represented the kind of League endeavour with which Americans could fully co-operate. It treated armaments as the cause rather than the symptom of conflict and divorced the issues of armaments from the world of politics. Hoover's proposal, a document into which the President had put many hours of intense, personal effort, was yet another example of the prevalent belief that the problem of war could be solved through the magic formulae of arms reduction. As such it is a period piece, one with the Kellogg Pact, that seems not a mere generation but ages removed from the world that was born out of the mushroom cloud over Hiroshima (6).

But the Republicans of the 1920s did initiate new approaches to Latin America; indeed, the basic foundations of the much publicised Good Neighbor policy of the 1930s were firmly established in the Republican era. After 1921 the United States began to retreat from the practice of direct military and political intervention and to accept, albeit haltingly, the principle of non-intervention in Latin affairs. While Hughes and Kellogg initiated the new approaches, it was the Hoover administration that produced the first coherent statement of the emerging policy by publishing the so-called 'Clark memorandum' of 1928. Clark, an official of the State Department, redefined the meaning of the Monroe Doctrine and purged from it the now heretical interventionism of the 'Roosevelt corollary'(7).

1 Treaty between the United States and Germany

The United States of America and Germany

Considering that the United States, acting in conjunction with its co-belligerents, entered into an Armistice with Germany on November 11, 1918, in order that a Treaty of Peace might be concluded;

Considering that the Treaty of Versailles was signed on June 28, 1919, and came into force according to the terms of its Article 440, but has not been ratified by the United States;

Considering that the Congress of the United States passed a Joint Resolution, approved by the President July 2, 1921, which reads in part as follows:

'*Resolved by the Senate and House of Representatives of the United States of America in Congress Assembled*, That the state of war declared to exist between the Imperial German Government and the United States of America by the joint resolution of Congress approved April 6, 1917, is hereby declared at an end.

'Sec. 2. That in making this declaration, and as a part of it, there are expressly reserved to the United States of America and its nationals any and all rights, privileges, indemnities, reparations, or advantages, together with the right to enforce the same, to which it or they have become entitled under the terms of the armistice signed November 11, 1918, or any extensions or modifications thereof; or which were acquired by or are in the possession of the United States of America by reason of its participation in the war or to which its nationals have thereby become rightfully entitled; or which, under the treaty of Versailles, have been stipulated for its or their benefit; or to which it is entitled as one of the principal allied and associated powers; or to which it is entitled by virtue of any Act or Acts of Congress; or other wise. . . .

Article I

Germany undertakes to accord to the United States, and the United States shall have and enjoy, all the rights, privileges, indemnities, reparations or advantages specified in the aforesaid Joint Resolution of the Congress of the United States of July 2, 1921, including all the rights and advantages stipulated for the benefit of the United States in the Treaty of Versailles which the United States shall fully enjoy notwithstanding the fact that such Treaty has not been ratified by the United States.

ARTICLE II

With a view to defining more particularly the obligations of Germany under the foregoing Article with respect to certain provisions in the Treaty of Versailles, it is understood and agreed between the High Contracting Parties:

(1) That the rights and advantages stipulated in that Treaty for the benefit of the United States, which it is intended the United States shall have and enjoy, are those defined in Section 1, of Part IV, and Parts V, VI, VIII, IX, X, XI, XII, XIV, and XV . . .

(2) That the United States shall not be bound by the provisions of Part I of that Treaty, nor by any provisions of that Treaty including those mentioned in Paragraph (1) of this Article, which relate to the Covenant of the League of Nations, nor shall the United States be bound by any action taken by the League of Nations, or by the Council or by the Assembly thereof, unless the United States shall expressly give its assent to such action. . . .

(4) That, while the United States is privileged to participate in the Reparation Commission, according to the terms of Part VIII of that Treaty, and in any other Commission established under the Treaty or under any agreement supplemental thereto, the United States is not bound to participate in any such commission unless it shall elect to do so. . . .

Papers Relating to the Foreign Relations of the United States, 1921, Vol. II (Washington, 1936), pp. 29-32 (excerpts)

2 Economic and Foreign Policy

(a) *Flotation of Foreign Loans. Press release issued by the Department of State, March 3, 1922*

At a conference held last summer between the President, certain members of the Cabinet and a number of American investment bankers, the interest of the Government in the public flotation of issues of foreign bonds in the American market was informally discussed and the desire of the Government to be duly and adequately informed regarding such transactions before their consummation, so that it might express itself regarding them if that should be requested or seem desirable, was fully explained. Subsequently the President was informed by the bankers that they and their associates were in harmony with the Government's wishes and would act accordingly.

The desirability of such cooperation, however, does not seem sufficiently well understood in banking and investment circles.

The flotation of foreign bond issues in the American market is assuming an increasing importance and on account of the bearing of such operations upon the proper conduct of affairs, it is hoped that American concerns that contemplate making foreign loans will inform the Department of State in due time of the essential facts and of subsequent developments of importance. Responsible American bankers will be competent to determine what information they should furnish and when it should be supplied.

American concerns that wish to ascertain the attitude of the Department regarding any projected loan should request the Secretary of State, in writing, for an expression of the Department's views. The Department will then give the matter consideration and, in the light of the information in its possession, endeavor to say whether objection to the loan in question does or does not exist, but it should be carefully noted that the absence of a statement from the Department, even though the Department may have been fully informed, does not indicate either acquiescence or objection. The Department will reply as promptly as possible to such inquiries.

The Department of State can not, of course, require American bankers to consult it. It will not pass upon the merits of foreign loans as business propositions, nor assume any responsibility whatever in connection with loan transactions. Offers for foreign loans should not, therefore, state or imply that they are contingent upon an expression from the Department of State regarding them, nor should any prospectus or contract refer to the attitude of this Government. The Department believes that in view of the possible national interests involved it should have the opportunity of saying to the underwriters concerned, should it appear advisable to do so, that there is or is not objection to any particular issue.

Papers Relating to the Foreign Relations of the United States, 1922, Vol. I (Washington, 1938), pp. 557–8

(b) *Reparations and the Origins of the Dawes Plan: Address by Secretary of State Hughes to the American Historical Association, December 29, 1922*

. . . The economic conditions in Europe give us the greatest concern. They have long received the earnest consideration of the administration.

It is idle to say that we are not interested in these problems, for we are deeply interested from an economic standpoint, as our credits and markets are involved, and from a humanitarian standpoint, as the heart of the American people goes out to those who are in distress. We cannot dispose of these problems by calling them European, for they are world problems and we cannot escape the injurious consequences of a failure to settle them.

They are, however, European problems in the sense that they cannot be solved without the consent of European governments. We cannot consent for them. The key to the settlement is in their hands, not in ours.

The crux of the European situation lies in the settlement of reparations. There will be no adjustment of other needs, however pressing, until a definite and accepted basis for the discharge of reparation claims has been fixed. It is futile to attempt to erect any economic structure in Europe until the foundation is laid.

How can the United States help in this matter? We are not seeking reparations. . . . We are bearing our own burden and through our loans a large part of Europe's burden in addition. No demands of ours stand in the way of a proper settlement of the reparations question.

Of course we hold the obligations of European governments and there has been much discussion abroad and here with respect to them. There has been a persistent attempt ever since the Armistice to link up the debts owing to our government with reparations or with projects of cancellation. This attempt was resisted in a determined manner under the former administration and under the present administration. The matter is plain enough from our standpoint. The capacity of Germany to pay is not at all affected by any indebtedness of any of the Allies to us. That indebtedness does not diminish Germany's capacity, and its removal would not increase her capacity. For example, if France had been able to finance her part in the war without borrowing at all from us, that is, by taxation and internal loans, the problem of what Germany could pay would be exactly the same. . . .

But what is our attitude toward the question of reparations, standing as it does as a distinct question and as one which cannot be settled unless the European governments concerned are able to agree?

We have no desire to see Germany relieved of her responsibility for the war or of her just obligations to make reparation for the injuries due to her aggression. There is not the slightest desire that France shall lose any part of her just claims. On the other hand, we do not wish to see a prostrate Germany. There can be no economic recuperation in Europe unless Germany recuperates. There will be no permanent peace unless economic satisfactions are enjoyed. There must be hope and industry must have promise of reward if there is to be prosperity. We should view with disfavor measures which instead of producing reparations would threaten disaster.

Some of our own people have suggested that the United States should assume the rôle of arbiter. There is one sufficient answer to this suggestion, and that is that we have not been asked to assume the rôle of arbiter. There could be no such arbitrament unless it were invited, and it would be an extraordinary and unprecedented thing for us to ask for such an invitation.

I do not think that we should endeavor to take such a burden of responsibility. We have quite enough to bear without drawing to ourselves all the ill feeling which would result from disappointed hopes and a settlement which would be viewed as forced upon nations by this country which at the same time is demanding the payment of the debts owing to it.

But the situation does call for a settlement upon its merits. The first condition of a satisfactory settlement is that the question should be taken out of politics. Statesmen have their difficulties, their public opinion, the exigencies which they must face. It is devoutly to be hoped that they will effect a settlement among themselves and that the coming meeting at Paris will find a solution. But if it does not, what should be done? The alternative of forcible measures to obtain reparations is not an attractive one. No one can foretell the extent of the serious consequences which might ensue from such a course. Apart from political results, I believe that the opinion of experts is that such measures will not produce reparation payments but might tend to destroy the basis of those payments which must be found in economic recuperation.

If, however, statesmen cannot agree and such an alternative is faced, what can be done? Is there not another way out? The fundamental condition is that in this critical moment the merits of the question, as an economic one, must alone be disregarded; mutual recriminations are of no avail; reviews of the past, whether accurate or inaccurate, promise nothing; assertions of blame on the one hand and excuses on the other come to naught.

There ought to be a way for statesmen to agree upon what Germany can pay, for no matter what claims may be made against her, that is the limit of satisfaction. There ought to be a way to determine that limit and to provide a financial plan by which immediate results can be obtained and the European nations can feel that the foundation has been laid for their mutual and earnest endeavors to bring about the utmost prosperity to which the industry of their people entitle them.

If statesmen cannot agree, and exigencies of public opinion make their course difficult, then there should be called to their aid those who can point the way to a solution.

Why should they not invite men of the highest authority in finance in their respective countries – men of such prestige, experience and honor that their agreement upon the amount to be paid, and upon a financial plan for working out the payments, would be accepted throughout the world as the most authoritative expression obtainable? Governments need not bind themselves in advance to accept the recommendations, but they can at least make possible such an inquiry with their approval and free the men who may represent their country in such a commission from any responsibility to Foreign Offices and from any duty to obey political instructions. In other words, they may invite an answer to this difficult and pressing question from men of such standing and in such circumstances of freedom as will insure a reply prompted only by knowledge and conscience. I have no doubt that distinguished Americans would be willing to serve in such a commission. If governments saw fit to reject the recommendation upon which such a body agreed, they would be free to do so, but they would have the advantage of impartial advice and of an enlightened public opinion. Peoples would be informed, the question would be rescued from assertion and counter-assertion and the problem put upon its way to solution.

Charles Evans Hughes, *The Pathway of Peace* (New York, 1925), pp. 53-7 (excerpts)

3 Limitation of Naval Armament

Speech delivered by Secretary of State Charles Evans Hughes at the opening session of the Conference on Limitation of Armament at Washington, November 21, 1921

The President invited the governments of the British Empire, France, Italy, and Japan to participate in a conference on the subject of limitation of armament, in connection with which Pacific and Far Eastern questions would also be discussed. It would have been most agreeable to the President to have invited all the Powers to take part in this Conference, but it was thought to be a time when other considerations should yield to the practical requirements of the existing exigency, and in this view the invitation was extended to the group known as the

Principal Allied and Associated Powers, which, by reason of the conditions produced by the war, control in the main the armament of the world. The opportunity to limit armament lies within their grasp.

It was recognized, however, that the interests of other Powers in the Far East made it appropriate that they should be invited to participate in the discussion of Pacific and Far Eastern problems, and, with the approval of the five Powers, an invitation to take part in the discussion of those questions has been extended to Belgium, China, the Netherlands, and Portugal.

The inclusion of the proposal for the discussion of Pacific and Far Eastern questions was not for the purpose of embarrassing or delaying an agreement for limitation of armament, but rather to support that undertaking by availing ourselves of this meeting to endeavor to reach a common understanding as to the principles and policies to be followed in the Far East and thus greatly to diminish, and if possible wholly to remove, discernible sources of controversy. . . .

In the public discussions which have preceded the Conference, there have been apparently two competing views; one, that the consideration of armament should await the result of the discussion of Far Eastern questions, and, another, that the latter discussion should be postponed until an agreement for limitation of armament has been reached. I am unable to find sufficient reason for adopting either of these extreme views. I think that it would be most unfortunate if we should disappoint the hopes which have attached to this meeting by a postponement of the consideration of the first subject. The world looks to this Conference to relieve humanity of the crushing burden created by competition in armament, and it is the view of the American government that we should meet that expectation without any unnecessary delay. It is therefore proposed that the Conference should proceed at once to consider the question of the limitation of armament.

This, however, does not mean that we must postpone the examination of Far Eastern questions. These questions of vast importance press for solution. It is hoped that immediate provision may be made to deal with them adequately, and it is suggested that it may be found to be entirely practicable through the distribution of the work among designated committees to make progress to the ends sought to be achieved without either subject being treated as a hindrance to the proper consideration and disposition of the other.

The proposal to limit armament by an agreement of the Powers is not a new one, and we are admonished by the futility of earlier efforts. . . .

[After summarizing the work of the two Hague conferences, Hughes continued]

This was the fruition of the efforts of eight years. Although the effect was clearly perceived, the race in preparation of armament, wholly unaffected by these futile suggestions, went on until it fittingly culminated in the greatest war of history; and we are now suffering from the unparalleled loss of life, the destruction of hopes, the economic dislocations, and the widespread impoverishment which measure the cost of the victory over the brutal pretensions of military force.

But if we are warned by the inadequacy of earlier endeavors for limitation of armament, we cannot fail to recognize the extraordinary opportunity now presented. We not only have the lessons of the past to guide us, not only do we have the reaction from the disillusioning experiences of war, but we must meet the challenge of imperative economic demands. What was convenient or highly desirable before is now a matter of vital necessity. If there is to be economic rehabilitation, if the longings for reasonable progress are not to be denied, if we are to be spared the uprisings of peoples made desperate in the desire to shake off burdens no longer endurable, competition in armament must stop. The present opportunity not only derives its advantage from a general appreciation of this fact, but the power to deal with the exigency now rests with a small group of nations, represented here, who have every reason to desire peace and to promote amity. The astounding ambition which lay athwart the promise of the Second Hague Conference no longer menaces the world, and the great opportunity of liberty-loving and peace-preserving democracies has come. Is it not plain that the time has passed for mere resolutions that the responsible Powers should examine the question of limitation of armament? We can no longer content ourselves with investigations, with statistics, with reports, with the circumlocution of inquiry. The essential facts are sufficiently known. The time has come, and this Conference has been called, not for general resolutions or mutual advice, but for action. We meet with full understanding that the aspirations of mankind are not to be defeated either by plausible suggestions of postponement or by impracticable counsels of perfection. Power and responsibility are here and the world awaits a practicable program which shall at once be put into execution. . . .

The question in relation to armament, which may be regarded as of primary importance at this time, and with which we can deal most promptly and effectively, is the limitation of naval armament. There are certain general considerations which may be deemed pertinent to this subject.

The first is that the core of the difficulty is to be found in the competition in naval programs, and that, in order appropriately to limit naval armament, competition in its production must be abandoned. Competition will not be remedied by resolves with respect to the method of its continuance. One program inevitably leads to another, and if competition continues, its regulation is impracticable. There is only one adequate way out and that is to end it now.

It is apparent that this cannot be accomplished without serious sacrifices. Enormous sums have been expended upon ships under construction and building programs which are now under way cannot be given up without heavy loss. Yet if the present construction of capital ships goes forward other ships will inevitably be built to rival them and this will lead to still others. Thus the race will continue so long as ability to continue lasts. The effort to escape sacrifices is futile. We must face them or yield our purpose.

It is also clear that no one of the naval Powers should be expected to make these sacrifices alone. The only hope of limitation of naval armament is by agreement among the nations concerned, and this agreement should be entirely fair and reasonable in the extent of the sacrifices required of each of the Powers. In considering the basis of such an agreement, and the commensurate sacrifices to be required, it is necessary to have regard to the existing naval strength of the great naval Powers, including the extent of construction already effected in the case of ships in process. This follows from the fact that one nation is as free to compete as another, and each may find grounds for its action. What one may do another may demand the opportunity to rival, and we remain in the thrall of competitive effort. I may add that the American delegates are advised by their naval experts that the tonnage of capital ships may fairly be taken to measure the relative strength of navies, as the provision for auxiliary combatant craft should sustain a reasonable relation to the capital ship tonnage allowed.

It would also seem to be a vital part of a plan for the limitation of naval armament that there should be a naval holiday. It is proposed that for a period of not less than ten years there should be no further construction of capital ships.

I am happy to say that I am at liberty to go beyond these general propositions and, on behalf of the American delegation acting under the instructions of the President of the United States, to submit to you a concrete proposition for an agreement for the limitation of naval armament.

It should be added that this proposal immediately concerns the

British Empire, Japan, and the United States. In view of the extraordinary conditions due to the World War affecting the existing strength of the navies of France and Italy, it is not thought to be necessary to discuss at this stage of the proceedings the tonnage allowance of these nations, but the United States proposes that this matter be reserved for the later consideration of the Conference.

In making the present proposal the United States is most solicitous to deal with the question upon an entirely reasonable and practicable basis, to the end that the just interests of all shall be adequately guarded and that national security and defense shall be maintained. Four general principles have been applied:

(1) That all capital ship-building programs, either actual or projected, should be abandoned;

(2) That further reduction should be made through the scrapping of certain of the older ships;

(3) That in general regard should be had to the existing naval strength of the Powers concerned;

(4) That the capital ship tonnage should be used as the measurement of strength for navies and a proportionate allowance of auxiliary combatant craft prescribed. . . .

The total reduction of tonnage on vessels existing, laid down, or for which material has been assembled (taking the tonnage of the new ships when completed), would be 448,928 tons.

Thus under this plan there would be immediately destroyed, of the navies of the three Powers, 66 capital fighting ships, built and building, with a total tonnage of 1,878,043.

It is proposed that it should be agreed by the United States, Great Britain, and Japan that their navies, with respect to capital ships, within three months after the making of the agreement shall consist of certain ships designated in the proposal and numbering for the United States 18, for Great Britain 22, for Japan, 10.

The tonnage of these ships would be as follows: Of the United States, 500,650; of Great Britain, 604,450; of Japan 299,700. In reaching this result, the age factor in the case of the respective navies has received appropriate consideration.

Replacement:

With respect to replacement, the United States proposes:

(1) That it be agreed that the first replacement tonnage shall not be laid down until 10 years from the date of the agreement:

(2) That replacement be limited by an agreed maximum of capital ship tonnage as follows:

For the United States . .	500,000 tons
For Great Britain	500,000 tons
For Japan	300,000 tons

(3) That subject to the 10-year limitation above fixed and the maximum standard, capital ships may be replaced when they are 20 years old by new capital ship construction;

(4) That no capital ship shall be built in replacement with a tonnage displacement of more than 35,000 tons.

I have sketched the proposal only in outline, leaving the technical details to be supplied by the formal proposition which is ready for submission to the delegates. . . .

With the acceptance of this plan the burden of meeting the demands of competition in naval armament will be lifted. Enormous sums will be released to aid the progress of civilization. At the same time the proper demands of national defense will be adequately met and the nations will have ample opportunity during the naval holiday of 10 years to consider their future course. Preparation for offensive naval war will stop now.

Charles Evans Hughes, *The Pathway of Peace*, pp. 20–31 (excerpts)

4 The United States and the League of Nations

(a) *The Problems of the American Minister to Switzerland: Excerpts from the diary of Joseph C. Grew*

To Leland Harrison, Assistant Secretary of State, from Hancock, N.H., August 10, 1922

. . . After my talk with the Secretary I find that my attitude towards the League will have to be exactly the same as before, and that it will not be possible to establish any more open connection than formerly. I had hoped to be authorized to play the role of an unofficial observer, openly . . . but while the Secretary left the matter to my discretion, he emphasized the importance of avoiding publicity, and I cannot therefore run the risk of visiting the League's offices or of openly moving to Geneva during sessions of the Council or other bodies, although this would have enabled me to keep the Department more closely and fully informed. . . .

Berne, Monday, September 11 [*1922*]

. . . In the course of the morning a pouch came in from Washington containing instructions which necessitated my going to Geneva too, so I took the 2.35 train, arriving at 5.35. . . .

On arriving at Geneva I took a taxi and stopped at the entrance of the League of Nations building to pick up Sweetser to motor out to Genthod together. We had arranged this by telephone as he was too busy to meet me elsewhere. I have always carefully avoided the League premises but it seemed safe enough merely to stop at the entrance to call for somebody. As luck, or ill-luck, would have it, the first person I ran into there was Henry Wales of the *Chicago Tribune*. . . . He said: 'Hello, what are *you* doing here! Looking into the Arms Traffic Commission?' I replied that I was there in a purely personal capacity, was visiting friends in the country and had stopped to see Sweetser, an old friend. I asked him not to say anything about it as there was no news in it and it would embarrass me greatly. . . . When I saw Sweetser he thought the chances were decidely in favor of Wales making a story of it. . . . I felt pretty uneasy during the next two days, but when the *Chicago Tribune* came from Paris two days later, there was not a word about my presence. . . .

Tuesday, September 12 [*1922*]

Sweetser called for me at 9.30 and motored me in to town and we walked for half an hour on the Quai Mont Blanc, discussing Austria, Mandates, Arms Traffic, Anatolia, etc. He told me much inside information which has not appeared either in the press or the *Journal* of the League, all of which was of value and enabled me to write several despatches on my return to Berne. I gave him some official American statistics for use by the League and took up with him a complaint by the Department that previous statistics had either not been used at all or had been published incorrectly. He will investigate. . . .

Then to the Consulate where I talked with Lewis Haskell and Robert Macatee [Consuls], then took a walk with Markus d'Oldenburg [Danish Minister to Switzerland], who tried to persuade me to stay for a dinner he was giving the same evening for Edward Benes, Prime Minister of Czechoslovakia. It would be decidedly interesting if Alice and I could stay openly in Geneva during meetings of the Assembly and the Council and see all these people, but that unfortunately is at present out of the question. . . .

Joseph C. Grew, *Turbulent Era*, ed. Walter Johnson, Vol. I (Boston, 1952), pp. 460-1

(b) *The Rejection of the Geneva Protocol. Memorandum by Secretary of State Hughes of a conversation with the British Ambassador, January 5, 1925*

Geneva Protocol. The Ambassador said that he had received a private letter from Mr. Austen Chamberlain requesting him to take up with the Secretary the question of the Geneva Protocol. Mr. Chamberlain desired to know the views of this Government. It would seem that the putting into effect of the Protocol without modifications might leave the way open for the development of situations which would be embarrassing with respect to the relations between Great Britain and the United States. It was a cardinal point in British policy to maintain friendly relations with the United States and to cooperate with this Government wherever possible, and there might be interference with this policy if contingencies should arise in which through the operation of the Protocol the British Government was brought into opposition to the interests of the United States. On the other hand, it seemed to the British Government that it would not be well to throw out the Protocol entirely, for if this were done there would most probably be a continuance of competitive armament in Europe which the countries concerned could not afford. The only alternative to such a competition in armament with all its possible consequences would seem to be the adoption in some form of such an arrangement as the Geneva Protocol proposed. The British Government were seeking for modifications which might suit the purpose and would be very glad to know the position of the United States.

The Secretary said he should hardly care to make any answer for this Government to such a broad inquiry, involving important questions of future policies, without bringing the matter to the attention of the President, and this he would do at the first opportunity. He did not mind saying, however, as an informal expression of his personal views, that there were two aspects at least of the Geneva Protocol which might give concern to this Government. The Secretary said that if the Protocol were taken as having practical value and of actually portending what it set forth, there would appear to be a proposal of a concert against the United States, when the Powers joining in the Protocol considered that the United States had committed some act of aggression, although the United States might believe itself to be entirely justified in its action, and in fact be acting in accordance with its traditional policies. The Secretary said that he did not believe that such a concert would actually become effective but he supposed that the Protocol must be taken as it is written and in this view the United States would be compelled to view it with disfavor. The Secretary said there was another class of cases where the action of the United States itself might not be involved but that of some other country with which the United States had trade relations, and the action of the Powers who had joined in the Protocol might turn out to be inimical to the interests of the United States in such relations with the country in question.

The Ambassador said that he had not supposed that the first situation would actually arise and he really had in mind the second case that the Secretary had put. In other words, they might be called upon to blockade some country and come into antagonism to the interests of the United States in consequence. The Secretary said that there was one thing he believed could be depended upon, and that was that this Government from its very beginning had been insistent upon the rights of neutrals and would continue to maintain them. The Secretary did not believe any Administration, short of a treaty concluded and ratified, could commit the country against assertion of its neutral rights in case there should be occasion to demand their recognition. The Ambassador said that he believed that that was the situation and that that was the point which his Government had in view. The Secretary said that while the effect of the Protocol upon the interests of the United States in the contingencies suggested seemed to be quite obvious, the Government of the United States did not desire to be put in the position of taking action against the adoption of the Protocol. He had rather expected that situations similar to those which might arise in the view of the United States, would be in contemplation of other Governments and especially of the British Government, and he had not believed that the Protocol would become effective according to its present terms; that it was desired by this Government that if other Governments did not approve the Protocol, they should deal with the matter from the standpoint of their own interests and not put the responsibility upon the United States.

The Ambassador said that there had been nothing on the particular point in Mr. Chamberlain's letter, but it had occurred to him (the Ambassador) that possibly the result might be reached by a reservation on the part of the British Government; that they could reserve the right in any contingency to which the sanctions might apply to consult with any Power that was not a member of the League of Nations and make such arrangements as might be desirable in the light of such consultation. The Ambassador said that he had not worked out the phraseology but the idea occurred to him and it seemed to him that it might be a satisfactory solution.

The Secretary said that he could well understand the reasons which might lead the British Government to make such a reservation but that he thought it would be inadvisable to have anything said on the other side to the effect that an arrangement had been made in relation to the ratification of the Protocol which was satisfactory to the United States. The Secretary said that if any such statement or suggestion was made there would at once be inquiry here as to what understanding we had and why we had it and what right we had to have it, et cetera; that it would be a most unpleasant situation. The Secretary must emphasize the point, therefore, that whatever action the British Government took it must take on its own responsibility and while, as it seemed to the Secretary, they could appropriately envisage the possible contingencies of conflict with the interests of the United States and develop their course accordingly, they should not make any suggestion that the course they did take was taken pursuant to some understanding with the United States.

The Secretary said this was all he cared to say at present and he would talk over the matter with the President. . . .

Papers Relating to the Foreign Relations of the United States, 1925, Vol. I (Washington, 1940), pp. 16-18

5 The Kellogg-Briand Pact (Treaty of Paris)

(a) *Letter of Transmittal from President Calvin Coolidge to President Doumergue of France, August 26, 1928*

Washington, August 26, 1928

It gives me great pleasure and satisfaction to extend to you and through you to the representatives of the nations assembled in Paris my cordial congratulations on the successful outcome of the negotiations inaugurated by France and the United States for a treaty renouncing war as an instrument of national policy and pledging the signatories to seek only by peaceful means the settlement of differences which may arise between them.

The treaty to be signed in Paris had its inception in the proposal submitted last year by the Government of France to the Government of the United States. The idea of Monsieur Briand has been made world wide. I am confident that the simple provisions of this treaty will be accepted by all nations because I am sure there is everywhere a will for peace. It is a great forward step in the preservation of peaceful relations between the nations and therefore will, I know, prove to be a historic document in the history of civilization. It has been a privilege to the United States to contribute to the success of this movement, a satisfaction to have been associated with France and other peace loving nations in thus writing into international law one of the deepest aspirations of the human conscience.

CALVIN COOLIDGE

(b) *Text of Treaty*

Treaty Between the United States and Other Powers, Signed at Paris, August 27, 1928

THE PRESIDENT OF THE GERMAN REICH, THE PRESIDENT OF THE UNITED STATES OF AMERICA, HIS MAJESTY THE KING OF THE BELGIANS, THE PRESIDENT OF THE FRENCH REPUBLIC, HIS MAJESTY THE KING OF GREAT BRITAIN, IRELAND AND THE BRITISH DOMINIONS BEYOND THE SEAS, EMPEROR OF INDIA, HIS MAJESTY THE KING OF ITALY, HIS MAJESTY THE EMPEROR OF JAPAN, THE PRESIDENT OF THE REPUBLIC OF POLAND, THE PRESIDENT OF THE CZECHOSLOVAK REPUBLIC,

Deeply sensible of their solemn duty to promote the welfare of mankind;

Persuaded that the time has come when a frank renunciation of war as an instrument of national policy should be made to the end that the peaceful and friendly relations now existing between their peoples may be perpetuated;

Convinced that all changes in their relations with one another should be sought only by pacific means and be the result of a peaceful and orderly process, and that any signatory Power which shall hereafter seek to promote its national interests by resort to war should be denied the benefits furnished by this Treaty;

Hopeful that, encouraged by their example, all the other nations of the world will join in this humane endeavor and by adhering to the present Treaty as soon as it comes into force bring their peoples within the scope of its beneficient provisions, thus uniting the civilized nations of the world in a common renunciation of war as an instrument of their national policy;

Have decided to conclude a Treaty and for that purpose have appointed as their respective Plenipotentiaries: . . .who . . . have agreed upon the following articles:

ARTICLE I

The High Contracting Parties solemnly declare in the names of their respective peoples that they condemn recourse to war for the solution of international controversies, and renounce it as an instrument of national policy in their relations with one another.

ARTICLE II

The High Contracting Parties agree that the settlement or solution of all disputes or conflicts of whatever nature or of whatever origin they may be, which may arise among them, shall never be sought except by pacific means.

ARTICLE III

The present Treaty shall be ratified by the High Contracting Parties named in the Preamble in accordance with their respective constitutional requirements, and shall take effect as between them as soon as all their several instruments of ratification shall have been deposited at Washington.

This Treaty shall, when it has come into effect as prescribed in the preceding paragraph, remain open as long as may be necessary for adherence by all the other Powers of the world. Every instrument evidencing the adherence of a Power shall be deposited at Washington and the Treaty shall immediately upon such deposit become effective as between the Power thus adhering and the other Powers parties hereto.

It shall be the duty of the Government of the United States to furnish each Government named in the Preamble and every Government subsequently adhering to this Treaty with a certified copy of the Treaty and of every instrument of ratification or adherence. It shall also be the duty of the Government of the United States telegraphically to notify such Governments immediately upon the deposit with it of each instrument of ratification or adherence.

IN FAITH WHEREOF the respective Plenipotentiaries have signed this Treaty in the French and English languages both texts having equal force, and hereunto affix their seals.

Papers Relating to the Foreign Relations of the United States, 1928, Vol. I (Washington, 1942), pp. 153-8 (excerpts)

6 President Hoover's Proposal to the Geneva Disarmament Conference

To the Conference for the Reduction and Limitation of Armaments, Geneva, dispatched on June 18, 1932

. . . The time has come when we should cut through the brush and adopt some broad and definite method of reducing the overwhelming burden of armament which now lies upon the toilers of the world. This would be the most important world step that could be taken to expedite economic recovery. We must make headway against the mutual fear and friction arising out of war armament which kill human confidence throughout the world. We can still remain practical in maintaining an adequate self-defense among all nations; we can add to the assurances of peace and yet save the people of the world from ten to fifteen billions of wasted dollars during the next ten years.

I propose that the following principles should be our guide:

First: The Kellogg-Briand Pact, to which we are all signatories, can only mean that the nations of the world have agreed that they will use their arms solely for defense.

Second: This reduction should be carried out not only by broad general cuts in armaments but by increasing the comparative power of defense through decreases in the power of the attack.

Third: The armaments of the world have grown up in general mutual relation to each other. And, speaking generally, such relativity should be preserved in making reductions.

Fourth: The reductions must be real and positive. They must effect economic relief.

Fifth: There are three problems to deal with – land forces, air forces, and naval forces. They are all interconnected. No part of the proposals which I make can be dissociated one from the other.

Based on these principles, I propose that the arms of the world should be reduced by nearly one-third.

Land Forces. In order to reduce the offensive character of all land forces as distinguished from their defensive character, I propose . . . the abolition of all tanks, all chemical warfare, and all large mobile guns. This would not prevent the establishment or increase of fixed fortifications of any character for the defense of frontiers and sea-coasts. It would give an increased relative strength to such defenses as compared with the attack.

I propose furthermore that there should be a reduction of one-third in strength of all land armies over and above the police component.

The land armaments of many nations are considered to have two functions. One is the maintenance of internal order in connection with the regular police forces of the country. The strength required for this purpose has been called the 'police component.' The other function is defense against foreign attack. The additional strength required for this purpose has been called the 'defense component.' While it is not suggested that these different components should be separated, it is necessary to consider this division as to functions in proposing a practical plan of reduction in land forces. Under the Treaty of Versailles and the other peace treaties, the armies of Germany, Austria, Hungary, and Bulgaria were reduced to a size deemed appropriate for the maintenance of internal order, Germany being assigned 100,000 troops for a population of approximately 65,000,000 people. I propose that we should accept for all nations a basic police component of soldiers proportionate to the average which was thus allowed Germany and these other states. This formula, with necessary corrections for powers having colonial possessions, should be sufficient to provide for the maintenance of internal order by the nations of the world. Having analyzed these two components in this fashion, I propose as stated above that there should be a reduction of one-third in the strength of all land armies over and above the police component.

Air Forces. All bombing planes to be abolished. This will do away with the military possession of types of planes capable of attacks upon civil populations and should be coupled with the total prohibition of all systematic bombardment of civilians from the air.

Naval Forces. I propose that the treaty number and tonnage of battleships shall be reduced by one-third; that the treaty tonnage of aircraft carriers, cruisers, and destroyers shall be reduced by one-fourth; that the treaty tonnage of submarines shall be reduced by one-third, and that no nation shall retain a submarine tonnage greater than 35,000.

The relative strength of naval arms in battleships and aircraft carriers, as between the five leading naval powers, was fixed by the Treaty of Washington. The relative strength in cruisers, destroyers, and submarines was fixed, as between the United States, Great Britain and Japan, by the Treaty of London. For the purposes of this proposal, it is suggested that the French and Italian strength in cruisers and destroyers be calculated as though they had joined in the Treaty of London on a basis approximating the so-called accord of March 1, 1931. There are various technical considerations connected with these naval discussions which will be presented by the delegation.

General. The effect of this plan would be to effect an enormous saving in cost of new construction and replacements of naval vessels. It would also save large amounts in the operating expense in all nations of land, sea, and air forces. It would greatly reduce offensive strength compared to defensive strength in all nations.

These proposals are simple and direct. They call upon all nations to contribute something. The contribution here proposed will be relative and mutual. I know of nothing that would give more hope for humanity today than the acceptance of such a program with such minor changes as might be necessary. It is folly for the world to go on breaking its back over military expenditure and the United States is willing to take its share of responsibility by making definite proposals that will relieve the world.

Papers relating to the Foreign Relations of the United States, 1932, Vol. I (Washington, 1948), pp. 187-8

7 Memorandum on the Monroe Doctrine

By J. Reuben Clark, December 17, 1928

THE SECRETARY.

Herewith I transmit a Memorandum on the Monroe Doctrine, prepared by your direction, given a little over two months ago. . . .

The Doctrine, (thus) declared by Monroe, when reduced to its lowest terms covers—

(1) Future *colonization by any European powers* of the *American continents.*

(2) Any attempt by the *allied powers* to extend their political system *to any portion of this hemisphere*, or (in its second statement) *to any part of either continent.*

(3) Any interposition, *by any European power*, for the purpose of oppressing or controlling in any other manner the destinies of the Latin American Governments 'who have declared their independence and maintained it, and whose independence we have on great consideration and just principles acknowledged.'

(4) Noninterference by the United States with the existing colonies or dependencies of any European power.

(5) Policy of leaving Spanish American colonies and Spain to themselves in the hope that other powers will pursue the same course. . . .

It is of first importance to have in mind that Monroe's declaration in its terms, relates solely to the relationships between European states on the one side, and, on the other side, the American continents, the Western Hemisphere, and the Latin American Governments which on December 2, 1823, had declared and maintained their independence which we had acknowledged.

It is of equal importance to note, on the other hand, that the declaration does not apply to purely inter-American relations.

Nor does the declaration purport to lay down any principles that are to govern the interrelationship of the states of this Western Hemisphere as among themselves.

The Doctrine states a case of United States *vs.* Europe, not of United States *vs.* Latin America.

Such arrangements as the United States has made, for example, with Cuba, Santo Domingo, Haiti, and Nicaragua, are not within the Doctrine as it was announced by Monroe. They may be accounted for as the expression of a national policy which, like the Doctrine itself, originates in the necessities of security or self-preservation – a policy which was foreshadowed by Buchanan (1860) and by Salisbury (1895), and was outlined in what is known as the 'Roosevelt corollary' to the Monroe Doctrine (1905) in connection with the Dominican debt protocol of 1904; but such arrangements are not covered by the terms of the Doctrine itself. . . .

The Doctrine has been useful, and such indeed was the real motive of its announcement, and it will remain of such use that it should never be abandoned, as a forewarning to European powers as to what this country would regard, in a restricted field, as inimical to its safety. It has been equally useful to the Americas as forecasting our attitude towards certain international problems and relations in which they might be involved.

But, recalling that the Doctrine is based upon the recognized right of self-preservation, it follows (it is submitted) that by the specification of a few matters in the Doctrine, the United States has not surrendered its right to deal, as it may be compelled, and under the rules and principles of international law, with the many others which are unspecified as these may arise, which others might, indeed, have been included in the declaration with as much propriety, legally, as those which were mentioned. By naming either one act or a series of acts which challenges our self-preservation, we do not stop ourselves from naming others as they may arise; otherwise the mention of one such act would foreclose all others. The custom of nations shows that invoking the right as to one menace does not foreclose a power from invoking it as to others. . . .

The so-called 'Roosevelt corollary' was to the effect, as generally understood, that in case of financial or other difficulties in weak Latin American countries, the United States should attempt an adjustment thereof lest European Governments should intervene, and intervening should occupy territory – an act which would be contrary to the principles of the Monroe Doctrine. This view seems to have had its inception in some observations of President Buchanan in his message to Congress of December 3, 1860, and was somewhat amplified by Lord Salisbury in his note to Mr. Olney of November 6, 1895, regarding the Venezuelan boundary dispute.

As has already been indicated above, it is not believed that this corollary is justified by the terms of the Monroe Doctrine, however much it may be justified by the application of the doctrine of self-preservation.

These various expressions and statements, as made in connection with the situations which gave rise to them, detract not a little from the scope popularly attached to the Monroe Doctrine, and they relieve that Doctrine of many of the criticisms which have been aimed against it.

Finally, it should not be overlooked that the United States declined the overtures of Great Britain in 1823 to make a joint declaration regarding the principles covered by the Monroe Doctrine, or to enter into a conventional arrangement regarding them. Instead this Government determined to make the declaration of high national policy on its own responsibility and in its own behalf. The Doctrine is thus purely unilateral. The United States determines when and if the principles of the Doctrine are violated, and when and if violation is threatened. We alone determine what measures if any, shall be taken to vindicate the principles of the Doctrine, and we of necessity determine when the principles have been vindicated. No other power of the world has any relationship to, or voice in, the implementing of the principles which the Doctrine contains. It is our Doctrine, to be by us invoked and sustained, held in abeyance, or abandoned as our high international policy or vital national interests shall seem to us, and to us alone, to demand.

Memorandum on the Monroe Doctrine, prepared by J. Reuben Clark (Washington, 1930), pp. ix-xxv (excerpts)

II

SOVIET-AMERICAN RELATIONS, 1921–41

Since 1945 Soviet-American relations have formed the central thread of American foreign policy. In the 1920s – indeed, throughout the entire inter-war period – they comprised only a minor chapter which attracted the attention of relatively few American citizens, public or private. But the documents in this chapter illustrate at least a few relevant themes: for, example, the fact that the 'honeymoon' of 1941–5 was but a brief interlude in a longer history of troubled relations and that ever since the revolution of 1917 Americans have been raising essentially the same set of questions about how and in what ways the United States should react to the Soviet Union and Communism.

The Republicans of the 1920s wanted no part of Communism. When Secretary of State Hughes wrote to Samuel Gompers in 1923, he made it abundantly clear that capitalist America could have no meaningful association with the enemies of free enterprise. He laid down a firm policy of non-recognition which became the Republican policy and remained in force throughout the Hoover years (**1**).

There were always at least a few Americans who sympathised with or championed the Russian cause. Senator William E. Borah, Chairman of the Foreign Relations Committee and the very model of the political maverick, was almost a lone voice in the Senate when he argued that it was ridiculous for the United States to pretend that the Soviet Union did not exist (**2** (**a**)). However, it was not until the late twenties and early thirties – significantly, not until after the onset of the Depression and the virtual collapse of American foreign trade – that a sustained movement in favour of diplomatic recognition got under way. Ironically it was led by businessmen desperate for foreign markets, even Communist markets, who provided much of the momentum. The speech of James Mooney, a vice-president of the General Motors Corporation, typified the approach of the business leadership (**2b**).

Franklin D. Roosevelt, soon after his inauguration in 1933, opened talks with the Russians and in November exchanged a series of notes with the Soviets that produced the long-delayed recognition. Roosevelt's motives appear relatively uncomplicated; he seems to have been little influenced by the argument for commercial expansion and to have made his decision on the grounds that it was simply pointless to continue the outmoded, sterile non-recognition policy (3).

But Soviet-American relations got worse with recognition rather than better. FDR thought that he had secured a series of binding promises from the Russians – pledges to make repayments on the old Imperial government's wartime debts to the United States and to refrain from Communist activities within the United States. When the Russians proved unco-operative, disillusionment became rapid. The intemperate report from Ambassador William C. Bullitt in April 1936 demonstrates the increasing bitterness (4). And Bullitt, it should be added, was one of the few Americans who in 1919 had urged Wilson to seek an accord with the Soviets and throughout the twenties had consistently urged the policy of recognition.

By 1940, and especially after the Soviet attack on Finland, Russian-American relations had reached their nadir. The cold, disdainful prose of Secretary Hull's memorandum of February 1940 indicates that the United States regarded Stalin's Russia as no better than Hitler's Germany (5).

1 Letter from Charles Evans Hughes to Samuel Gompers

July 19, 1923

MY DEAR MR. GOMPERS: I have your letter of the ninth instant with respect to the grounds upon which the recognition of the present regime in Russia has been withheld.

You refer with just emphasis to the tyrannical exercise of power by this regime. The seizure of control by a minority in Russia came as a grievous disappointment to American democratic thought which had enthusiastically acclaimed the end of the despotism of the Czars and the entrance of free Russia into the family of democratic nations. Subsequent events were even more disturbing. The right of free speech and other civil liberties were denied. Even the advocacy of those rights which are usually considered to constitute the foundation of freedom was declared to be counter-revolutionary and punishable by death. Every form of political opposition was ruthlessly exterminated. There followed the deliberate destruction of the economic life of the country. Attacks were made not only upon property in its so-called capitalistic form, but recourse was had also to the requisitioning of labor. All voluntary organizations of workers were brought to an end. To unionize or strike was followed by the severest penalties. When labor retaliated by passive resistance, workmen were impressed into a huge labor army. The practical effect of this program was to plunge

Russia once more into medievalism. Politically there was a ruthless despotism and economically the situation was equally disastrous.

It is true that, under the pressure of the calamitous consequences, the governing group in Russia has yielded certain concessions. The so-called new economic policy permitted a partial return to economic freedom. The termination of forcible requisitions of grain has induced the peasantry to endeavor to build up production once more and favorable weather conditions have combined to increase the agricultural output. How far the reported exports of Russian grain are justified by the general economy of the country is at least an open question. Manufacturing industry has to a great extent disappeared. The suffrage, so far as it may be exercised, continues to be limited to certain classes and even among them the votes of some categories count more than the votes of others. A new constitution has just now been promulgated providing in effect for the continuance of the regime of the 1917 *coup d'état* under a new title. The Constitution, it is understood, contains no bill of rights, and the civil liberties of the people remain insecure. There is no press except the press controlled by the regime, and the censorship is far-reaching and stringent. Labor is understood to be still at the mercy of the State. While membership in official unions is no longer obligatory, workmen may not organize or participate in voluntary unions.

The fundamentals of the Russian situation are pretty generally understood in the United States and have made a profound impression upon the thought of our people. We are constantly made aware of this in the Department of State by the various ways in which public opinion makes itself felt in the seat of government. We learn of the hope of America that Russia should have the opportunity of free political expression and that she should be enabled to restore her economic life and regain prosperity and once more to take her place among the nations on the basis of mutual helpfulness and respect. There can be no question of the sincere friendliness of the American people toward the Russian people. And there is for this very reason a strong desire that nothing should be done to place the seal of approval on the tyrannical measures that have been adopted in Russia or to take any action which might retard the gradual reassertion of the Russian people of their right to live in freedom.

To the Department of State, charged with the conduct of our foreign relations, in accordance with the accepted principles of international intercourse, the problem presents itself necessarily in somewhat less general terms. We are not concerned with the question of the legitimacy of a government as judged by former European standards. We recognize the right of revolution and we do not attempt to determine the internal concerns of other States. The following words of Thomas Jefferson, in 1793, express a fundamental principle: 'We surely cannot deny to any nation that right whereon our own Government is founded, – that every one may govern itself according to whatever form it pleases, and change these forms at its own will; and that it may transact its business with foreign nations through whatever organ it thinks proper, whether king, convention, assembly, committee, president or anything else it may choose. The will of the nation is the only thing essential to be regarded.'...

But while a foreign regime may have securely established itself through the exercise of control and the submission of the people to, or their acquiescence in, its exercise of authority, there still remain other questions to be considered. Recognition is an invitation to intercourse. It is accompanied on the part of the new government by the clearly implied or express promise to fulfill the obligations of intercourse. These obligations include, among other things, the protection of the persons and property of the citizens of one country lawfully pursuing their business in the territory of the other and abstention from hostile propaganda by one country in the territory of the other. In the case of the existing regime in Russia, there has not only been the tyrannical procedure to which you refer, and which has caused the question of the submission or acquiescence of the Russian people to remain an open one, but also a repudiation of the obligations inherent in international intercourse and a defiance of the principles upon which alone it can be conducted....

What is most serious is that there is conclusive evidence that those in control at Moscow have not given up their original purpose of destroying existing governments wherever they can do so throughout the world. Their efforts in this direction have recently been lessened in intensity only by the reduction of the cash resources at their disposal. You are well aware from the experiences of the American Federation of Labor of this aspect of the situation which must be kept constantly in view. I had occasion to refer to it last March in addressing the Women's Committee for the Recognition of Russia. It is worth while to repeat the quotations which I then gave from utterances of the leaders of the Bolshevik Government on the subject of world revolution, as the authenticity of these has not been denied by their authors. Last November Zinoviev said, 'The eternal in the Russian revolution is the fact that it is the beginning of the world revolution.' Lenin, before the last Congress of the Third Internationale, last fall, said that 'the revolutionists of all countries must learn the organization, the planning, the method and the substance of revolutionary work.' 'Then, I am convinced,' he said, 'the outlook of the world revolution will not be good but excellent.' And Trotsky, addressing the Fifth Congress of the Russian Communist Youths at Moscow last October, – not two years ago but last October, – said this: 'That means, comrades, that revolution is coming in Europe as well as in America, systematically, step by step, stubbornly and with gnashing of teeth in both camps. It will be long protracted, cruel and sanguinary.'

The only suggestion that I have seen in answer to this portrayal of a fixed policy is that these statements express the views of the individuals in control of the Moscow regime rather than of the regime itself. We are unable, however, to find any reason for separating the regime, and its purpose from those who animate it, and control it, and direct it so as to further their aims.

While this spirit of destruction at home and abroad remains unaltered the question of recognition by our Government of the authorities at Moscow cannot be determined by mere economic considerations or by the establishment in some degree of a more prosperous condition, which of course we should be glad to note, or simply by a consideration of the probable stability of the regime in question. There cannot be intercourse among nations any more than among individuals except upon a general assumption of good faith. We would welcome convincing evidence of a desire of the Russian authorities to observe the fundamental conditions of international intercourse and the abandonment by them of the persistent attempts to subvert the institutions of democracy as maintained in this country and in others. It may confidently be added that respect by the Moscow regime for the liberties of other peoples will most likely be accompanied by appropriate respect for the essential rights and liberties of the Russian people themselves. The sentiment of our people is not deemed to be favorable to the acceptance into political fellowship of this regime so long as it denies the essential bases of intercourse and cherishes, as an ultimate and definite aim, the destruction of the free institutions which we have laboriously built up, containing as they do the necessary assurances of the freedom of labor upon which our prosperity must depend.

Papers Relating to the Foreign Relations of the United States, 1923, Vol. II (Washington, 1938), pp. 760–4

2 Advocates of Recognition

(a) *Excerpts from a speech in the Senate by Senator Borah, February 21, 1923*

. . . It can not be other than a menace to the peace of the entire world that a vast people, with vast natural resources and undoubtedly a great future, are outlawed among the nations. Prior to the war Russia comprised one-sixth of the entire land surface of the globe, and her mineral and timber wealth constituted the greatest undeveloped natural resources in the world.

I can understand why it is to the interest of certain powers in Europe to retard the development of Russia. It is not an interest with which I could have any possible sympathy; but, nevertheless, it is such an interest as has predominated to a marked degree in the foreign policies of European nations. I can understand why powers would organize to finance Denikine and Wrangel to break up and destroy the Russian Government or else restore the old régime, but that ought not to be a policy with which the United States could have any possible sympathy. It is not in the interest of humanity and it is certainly not in the interest of the material welfare of the people either of Russia or of the United States.

There seems to be a popular belief – I do not assume, of course, that it obtains in the State Department – that in recognizing a government we, in a measure, approve of the form of government which the people of that government may have at the time of the recognition. I have received an abundance of letters from people of more or less intelligence which say the recognition of Russia would set the stamp of approval by the United States upon that particular form of government which the Russian people are said at this time to have. Such recognition is not an approval or a disapproval of the form of government; it is a recognition of the fact that they have a government.

It is not an approval of their form of government, any more than our recognition of Turkey today is an approval of the Turkish form of government or of her acts under it. We, finding a people with a government which they have established, recognize as a fact that a government has been established and invite them to become members of the family of nations by the act of recognition. . . .

If we should decline to recognize Russia because of her form of government, and should carry that principle into practice it would necessarily require us to refuse recognition to or withdraw recognition from several nations which I might name.

So far, therefore, as the government from an internal standpoint is concerned, outside of the relationship which it may have with the governments of the earth in its foreign affairs, it is not of the slightest concern to the people of the United States or to the Government of the United States what kind of a government it is. If we shall find in this discussion that, notwithstanding its form of government, it is prepared to discharge its obligations to the other nations of the world, to meet the relationship, and in good faith to discharge the obligations which rest upon it, it is, I say, not of the slightest concern to us what their particular form of government may be. . . .

The present Russian Government has been in existence for six years; it has gone through the chaotic period; it is in the process of evolution; it represents authority; it represents at the present time the support of the Russian people. It is protecting life and property; it is transacting business with foreign nations; it is discharging every duty and obligation which rests upon a government, whether it be according to our idea of what a government should be or not; and if by our connivance or our failure to accord recognition it breaks down, we shall necessarily as a moral proposition become responsible in a large degree for what is to follow. Who is to take its place? Semenoff, or some representative of Wrangel, or some of the refugees whose interest in Russia is to see the old régime restored? In my humble opinion, the Russian peasant will suffer incalculable misery and go through years of turmoil before he will return to the old régime. Is it not infinitely better in a friendly way to undertake to bring Russia to the position which she ought to occupy under a sane and sound democratic form of government? For myself, sir, I do not want to see my Government connive at a policy which will add misery to that great people, which may bring on years of civil war, which may restore the old rule with all its incompetency and corruption and cruelty. Think for a moment what it all means. Let us forget for a time a few individuals and think of the mass of suffering humanity in case of another revolution or counter-revolution, the women and children who must pay with their lives for the wickedness of such a course. We are constantly saying officially we sympathize with the people of Russia. Is it not time to give evidence of that sympathy by deeds?

Let me digress to say that if it is true that they are engaged or would continue to be engaged in propaganda which is designed to present their view of government to the people of the United States, could we not more effectually deal with it if we were upon friendly relations with them than we can now? What possible reason would they have for continuing an unfriendly act upon their part toward this Government after amicable relations had been established, and it was to every interest of the Russian Government and the Russian people to build up the friendliest relations and to accentuate trade relations between the two Governments? They would have no occasion for continuing any such course; and in view of the fact that they have modified their communistic form of government entirely and completely from that which existed at the time the propaganda was going on, they would have no occasion, from the standpoint of an apostle to continue the advocacy of such doctrines.

I never have been able to understand the shivering fear which some people in this country entertain with reference to the effect of this propaganda from Russia or elsewhere. Whom is it going to hurt? I do not think it would affect the Senate. I do not think it would affect the House of Representatives. Whom are you afraid of – the farmer? It is the farmer in Russia who has destroyed or modified communism. It is the peasantry in Russia that represents individualism. It is the eighty-five per cent of people of Russia who have made that propaganda absolutely worthless and futile. You could pile your carloads of propaganda into the center of the agricultural population of the country and they would use it for fuel. Whom is it going to undermine?

Let me tell you. If you will take the tax burdens off the people of this country, if you will restore economic conditions so that they may have an adequate price for their products, if you will lift the burden which is crushing the people of the world through militarism and through armaments, there will be very little soil in which to sow the seeds of Bolshevism. Our conduct toward Russia has fed Bolshevism from the beginning. It has strengthened Lenin and Trotsky every day that it continued to exist, so I do not know what they would do; I do not care what they would do. I am perfectly willing to trust the American people against such propaganda. I do not know of any soil so sterile in which to sow and let die the seeds of Bolshevism as the common people of America. I will trust our people to deal with such propaganda.

William E. Borah, *American Problems* (New York, 1924), pp. 201-31 (excerpts)

(b) *Excerpts from a speech by James D. Mooney, a vice-president General Motors Corporation in 1931*

It is very difficult to find flaws in Russian economic thinking, as expressed in their actual plans and actions. Certainly they are very wise, for the long pull, in putting an embargo on consumer goods and importing only productive machinery, tools and equipment. They have been straining themselves, and taking some temporary punishment in their standards of living, by exporting wheat and oil and timber and even some manufactured goods, to establish credits to pay for tools. But isn't this commendable? We certainly approve of the man in our country who has the courage to make sacrifices in his own personal expenditures, so that he can put his money 'back into the business.'

A word about the Russian menace to American industry and agriculture. We Americans as consumers, as well as the rest of the world as consumers, cannot fail to benefit richly by the exploitation of Russia's great economic resources. Let's put the practical question: 'What are we going to do about the Russian menace anyway?' Shall we stop selling them machinery and equipment? I visited a great variety of mines and mills, factories and powerhouses in Russia and I saw very little machinery and equipment that could not be duplicated out of European countries, and that these countries would not be glad to sell Russia.

The fact is that Russia, particularly in her primary products, which, at least over the immediate period ahead, are the principal things she will have to sell, is in a position to furnish us some things which we need, and which she is in a better position to give us than we are able to supply ourselves. On the other hand, we have many things, particularly in our manufactured articles, which she needs, and which we are in the best position to supply. Obviously then the situation is solved to the best effect when we set up with Russia to trade in these things. There is no danger for us in this, providing it is intelligently handled. On the other hand, there is a great benefit to be derived. The real danger arises out of our present inclination to shut our eyes to the economics in the situation.

Really there is a strong analogy between what Russia is doing now in developing her primary resources and what we, ourselves, did in the early days along the same lines. Our country's development and prosperity have been based on the tremendous development of our own primary resources. All the rest of our development is predicated on that early movement. Russia is doing exactly what we did, and it should be easy for us to understand what she is doing.

I can summarize my own views, covering our economic and trade relationship with Russia, as follows: First, Russia is an excellent customer of the United States now, and our business with Russia can be remarkably expanded. Second, if we sell to Russia, we must be prepared to buy from her. The Russians quite naturally will insist on this as time goes on. Furthermore, for our own selfish interest, we must abandon the economic absurdity of being willing to ship goods to customers with the presumption that they can be paid for in anything but goods or services we accept from them.

Third, as traders, the complexion of Russia's political system, or system of government, should interest us no more than such complexions in any other of the many countries in which we do business. Fourth, the formal structure of the Russian government is well crystallized. There is a general emotional background supporting the structure. The political forces in the government are very cleverly carrying out a rigid indoctrination among the Russians everywhere that is resulting in a permanent 'set' of the government institutions that have been established. These conditions are all indicative of permanency and stability in the government. Fifth, Russia is a good credit risk. Her great resources and her aggressive economic program will provide the capacity to pay her bills. Russia's will to pay has been evidenced by her good credit history, and she has every reason to guard her excellent credit record.

Economic Review of the Soviet Union, Vol. VI, No. 10 (May 15, 1931), pp. 223-4

3 Recognition of the Soviet Union

Three Messages fram President Franklin D. Roosevelt to Maxim Litvinov, Soviet Commisar for Foreign Affairs, November 16, 1933

(a)

MY DEAR MR. LITVINOV: I am glad to have received the assurance expressed in your note to me of this date that it will be the fixed policy of the Government of the Union of Soviet Socialist Republics:

(1) To respect scrupulously the indisputable right of the United States to order its own life within its own jurisdiction in its own way and to refrain from interfering in any manner in the internal affairs of the United States, its territories or possessions.

(2) To refrain, and to restrain all persons in government service and all organizations of the Government or under its direct or indirect control, including the organizations in receipt of any financial assistance from it, from any act overt or covert liable in any way whatsoever to injure the tranquility, prosperity, order, or security of the whole or

any part of the United States, its territories or possessions, and in particular, from any act tending to incite or encourage armed intervention, or any agitation or propaganda having as an aim, the violation of the territorial integrity of the United States, its territories or possessions, or the bringing about by force of a change in the political or social order of the whole or any part of the United States, its territories or possessions.

(3) Not to permit the formation or residence on its territory of any organization or group – and to prevent the activity on its territory of any organization or group, or of representatives or officials of any organization or group – which makes claim to be the Government of, or makes attempt upon the territorial integrity of, the United States, its territories or possessions; not to form, subsidize, support or permit on its territory military organizations or groups having the aim of armed struggle against the United States, its territories or possessions, and to prevent any recruiting on behalf of such organizations and groups.

(4) Not to permit the formation or residence on its territory of any organization or group – and to prevent the activity on its territory of any organization or group, or of representatives or officials of any organization or group – which has as an aim the overthrow or the preparation for the overthrow of, or the bringing about by force of a change in, the political or social order of the whole or any part of the United States, its territories or possessions.

It will be the fixed policy of the Executive of the United States within the limits of the powers conferred by the Constitution and the laws of the United States to adhere reciprocally to the engagements above expressed.

(b)

MY DEAR MR. LITVINOV: As I have told you in our recent conversations, it is my expectation that after the establishment of normal relations between our two countries many Americans will wish to reside temporarily or permanently within the territory of the Union of Soviet Socialist Republics, and I am deeply concerned that they should enjoy in all respects the same freedom of conscience and religious liberty which they enjoy at home.

As you well know, the Government of the United States, since the foundation of the Republic, has always striven to protect its nationals, at home and abroad, in the free exercise of liberty of conscience and religious worship, and from all disability or persecution on account of their religious faith or worship. And I need scarcely point out that the rights enumerated below are those enjoyed in the United States by all citizens and foreign nationals and by American nationals in all the major countries of the world.

The Government of the United States, therefore, will expect that nationals of the United States of America within the territory of the Union of Soviet Socialist Republics will be allowed to conduct without annoyance or molestation of any kind religious services and rites of a ceremonial nature, including baptismal, confirmation, communion, marriage and burial rites, in the English language, or in any other language which is customarily used in the practice of the religious faith to which they belong, in churches, houses, or other buildings appropriate for such service, which they will be given the right and opportunity to lease, erect or maintain in convenient situations.

We will expect that nationals of the United States will have the right to collect from their co-religionists and to receive from abroad voluntary offerings for religious purposes; that they will be entitled without restriction to impart religious instruction to their children, either singly or in groups, or to have such instruction imparted by persons whom they may employ for such purpose; that they will be given and protected in the right to bury their dead according to their religious customs in suitable and convenient places established for that purpose, and given the right and opportunity to lease, lay out, occupy and maintain such burial grounds subject to reasonable sanitary laws and regulations.

We will expect that religious groups or congregations composed of nationals of the United States of America in the territory of the Union of Soviet Socialist Republics will be given the right to have their spiritual needs ministered to by clergymen, priests, rabbis or other ecclesiastical functionaries who are nationals of the United States of America, and that such clergymen, priests, rabbis or other ecclesiastical functionaries will be protected from all disability or persecution and will not be denied entry into the territory of the Soviet Union because of their ecclesiastical status.

(c)

MY DEAR MR. LITVINOV: I am very happy to inform you that as a result of our conversations the Government of the United States has decided to establish normal diplomatic relations with the Government of the Union of Soviet Socialist Republics and to exchange ambassadors.

I trust that the relations now established between our peoples may forever remain normal and friendly, and that our nations henceforth may cooperate for their mutual benefit and for the preservation of the peace of the world.

Papers Relating to the Foreign Relations of the United States to The Soviet Union, 1933–1939 (Washington, 1952), pp. 27-30

4 The Disillusionment of an American in Moscow

Message of Ambassador William C. Bullitt to Secretary Hull, April 20, 1936

SIR: I have the honor to submit my views as to the policies the United States should follow with respect to the Soviet Union and Communism. . . .

. . . . .

Today Stalin considers it sound strategy to support democratic forms of government in countries in which communism is still weak; but the meaning of that support was displayed by Dimitrov at the Comintern Congress in August, 1935, when he pointed out that at the moment the cause of communism could be promoted best by use of the tactics of the Trojan horse and warned his communist comrades that they were not good communists if they felt that it was indecent or unduly hypocritical to become the collaborators and pretended friends of democrats in order the better eventually to lead those democrats to the firing squad.

The problem of relations with the Government of the Soviet Union is, therefore, a subordinate part of the problem presented by communism as a militant faith determined to produce world revolution and the 'liquidation', (that is to say, murder), of all non-believers.

There is no doubt whatsoever that all orthodox communist parties in all countries, including the United States, believe in mass murder. Moreover, the loyalty of a believing communist is not to the nation of which he is technically a citizen but to his faith and to the Caliph of that faith. To such men the most traitorous betrayals are the highest virtues.

In the history of the human race many nations have had to deal with citizens whose loyalty lay beyond the boundaries of their native land. To deal with such men by means of secret police and firing squads is traditional. But to deal with them while preserving the liberties which have been gained so painfully by western peoples since the Middle Ages is extraordinarily difficult. To adopt the methods of the Nazis is to sacrifice the freedom from fear of the State which is among the most precious conquests of civilization, and to slay our heritage in attempting to defend it.

Yet it must be recognized that communists are agents of a foreign power whose aim is not only to destroy the institutions and liberties of our country, but also to kill millions of Americans. Our relations with the Soviet Union, therefore, involve questions of domestic policy which can not be answered except on the basis of a careful estimate of the strength of world communism and the reality or unreality of its threat to our liberties and lives. . . .

Papers relating to the Foreign Relations of the United States to the Soviet Union, 1933–1939 (Washington, 1952), pp. 291–2.

5 The Nadir of Soviet-American Relations

Memorandum of a Conversation between Secretary Hull and the Soviet Ambassador, February 1, 1940

The Soviet Ambassador came in at his own request. He said he had two points to bring up, one relating to a personal matter and the other to the interference of trade between our two countries.

The Ambassador drew out a manuscript of the recent speech of Assistant Secretary of War Louis Johnson on January fifteenth before the New York State Bankers Association in New York City, and proceeded very vigorously to condemn the criticism in the speech of totalitarian countries, and especially the comparison between Finnish soldiers and Soviet soldiers, greatly to the disadvantage of the latter. He made bitter complaint. I then proceeded to say that he must realize that statesmen and officials in his country, and particularly the government-controlled press, including *Pravda*, have been in the habit of applying almost every sort of epithet to the United States and to our officials and statesmen, but that this action has been passed unnoticed here. The Ambassador must understand, however, that this habit of applying epithets in his country has naturally created a general feeling here that, if persons in the United States should occasionally talk back in similar language, the Soviet Government, having set the example, ought not to think of making complaint. He sought to palliate and in effect to deny my statements about these practices in his country. I adhered to my contention. Furthermore, I said that when the American Minister and well-known and trusted American newspaper correspondents in Finland send unequivocal reports back to this Government to the effect that Russian bombers are killing numerous unarmed men, women and children in Finland, the Soviet Government must realize that people in a country like the United States or in most countries will insist on voicing the bitter feeling they entertain in regard to such assassinations and that no one can control them in this respect even if they should so desire. I added that this was another phase of the situation that might well be considered in connection with the utterance of Colonel Johnson, which, by the way, I stated I had not seen. The Ambassador sought to deny any bombing of civilians from the air, but I insisted that the evidence of our Government was beyond any contradiction from such a round-about way as Moscow.

The Ambassador then took up the alleged breach of the gasoline contract between American citizens and Soviet agencies somewhat like the one pending with Japan. My replies and comments on this subject were similar to those I made to the Japanese Ambassador on January thirty-first. This included a reminder of how the Soviet Government had violated contracts and agreements with this Government. In particular, I mentioned the agreement entered into at the time of Russian recognition by this Government and enumerated a number of very indefensible acts and practices toward this Government and its citizens by the Soviet Government or under its authority. The Ambassador sought to palliate these statements but without any serious attempt. He stated that this country was retaliating with respect to all trade relations between the two countries, even including a refusal to lease American ships to the Soviet Government for commercial transportation.

I again referred to the general state of lawlessness existing in so many parts of the world and unprovoked fighting going on for purposes of conquest, and said that, in the general state of turmoil and violation of all agreements and laws, anything may happen with the result that this country is more or less on a day-to-day basis with regard to many of its methods and practices, until such fighting slows down. At this point I was called in to the press conference and the Ambassador said that he was virtually through and would not remain.

Papers Relating to the Foreign Relations of the United States, 1940, Vol. 5 (Washington, 1958), pp. 250–1

III

THE FAR EAST: FROM MANCHURIA TO PEARL HARBOR

World War II came to America with great suddenness out of the Hawaiian dawn on Sunday, December 7, 1941 when Japanese carrier aircraft struck a still slumbering Pearl Harbor. Thirty minutes of Japanese bombing smashed the battleships of the American fleet and destroyed the foundations of American isolation.

The attack on Pearl Harbor came without warning, but tensions had been building between Japan and America for a decade. Conflict had been a distinct possibility since Japan had signed the Tripartite Pact with Germany and Italy in the late summer of 1940. The various documents in this chapter single out notable turning-points in the long, tortuous road to Pearl Harbor.

The first signs of potential discord became visible in 1931 when Japan moved into Manchuria. Her action indicated that the elaborate treaty structure of the Washington Conference had lost its relevance. While Europe expressed relatively little concern, it was, ironically, the supposedly isolationist United States that was most disturbed by Japan's military acts. American policy was by no means heroic or daring. After a mild political flirtation with the League of Nations (important as marking the first time that America had recognised the political activities of the League), the Hoover administration settled for the non-recognition policy spelled out in Secretary of State Stimson's letter to Senator Borah (1). Non-recognition solved nothing. It was, literally, a substitute for policy, and it exacerbated Japanese-American relations with its moral fervour. Still, it was the only one of Hoover's foreign policies that Franklin Roosevelt carried forth after 1933 as well as a clear sign of American opposition to the Japanese thrust on the mainland of Asia.

In 1937, at the Marco Polo bridge, again in Manchuria, fighting erupted between China and Japan. The Asian phase of World War II had begun. At the urging of Secretary Hull, President Roosevelt decided that the time had come to warn America of growing international dangers. He therefore turned a utine political speech at Chicago, Illinois, into one of his most famous addresses – the 'Quarantine the Aggressors' speech of October 5, 1937 (2). Though his metaphor was cloudy (and, indeed, was never clarified), FDR's speech implied that the United States was about to become an active participant in world politics. But the public outcry was immediate and deafening. Roosevelt retreated, ruefully telling one of his advisers that it was a terrible thing, when you were trying to lead a nation, to look over your shoulder and find no one there. Hence, when the nations which had signed the Nine Power Pact of 1922 met in Brussels in November to debate what if any action to take, Hull's instructions to the American delegate, Norman Davis, made it clear that the United States was not prepared to lead any movement against Japan (3). Thus the Quarantine Speech stands not as a significant change in basic American policy but simply as a milestone in the evolution of Roosevelt's own thinking – the point when he made his personal break with isolation.

In the autumn of 1940 Japan signed on as a treaty partner with Germany and Italy. The spectre of unified action by the Axis had an immediate effect upon American opinion but nowhere did the Japanese decision produce a stronger impact than within the American embassy in Tokyo. Joseph Clark Grew, a career Foreign Service officer and Ambassador to Japan since 1932, was a man who had been appalled by the implications of the Quarantine Speech and who had long counselled prudence and moderation in dealing with the Japanese. But he now concluded that the United States must resist Japan's advances with greater firmness. His 'Green Light' message of September 12, 1940, was perhaps the most significant of all the dispatches which Grew sent to Washington during his ten years in Japan (4).

1941 brought further Japanese advances. But the United States had decided that Hitler's Germany was the greater immediate menace and therefore chose to avoid a direct confrontation with Japan while Hitler remained unchecked. Then in midsummer of 1941 Japan moved into French Indo-China, and the Roosevelt administration, after long and often bitter debate, decided that it could no longer delay the imposition of a final embargo upon the shipment of oil and petroleum products to Japan (5 (a), 5 (b)). This, in retrospect, was the critical decision – for the Japanese, now threatened with an impending and potentially crippling oil shortage, concluded that they must either achieve a final diplomatic settlement with the United States within weeks or go to war. The final negotiations which followed were, in every sense, both futile and anticlimactic. Japan and the United States presented each other with proposals that were completely unacceptable (6 (a), 6 (b)). When the final American note of November 26 was received in Tokyo, the Japanese carrier fleet was already headed eastwards across the Pacific to its rendezvous off Hawaii.

1 The Manchurian Crisis

Letter from Secretary of State Henry L. Stimson to Senator William E. Borah, February 23, 1932

MY DEAR SENATOR BORAH:
You have asked my opinion whether, as has been sometimes recently suggested, present conditions in China have in any way indicated that the so-called Nine Power Treaty has become inapplicable or ineffective or rightly in need of modification, and if so, what I considered should be the policy of this Government.

This Treaty, as you of course know, forms the legal basis upon which now rests the 'Open Door' policy towards China. That policy, enunciated by John Hay in 1899, brought to an end the struggle among various powers for so-called spheres of interest in China which was threatening the dismemberment of that empire. To accomplish this Mr. Hay invoked two principles (1) equality of commercial opportunity among all nations in dealing with China, and (2) as necessary to that equality the preservation of China's territorial and administrative integrity. These principles were not new in the foreign policy of America. They had been the principles upon which it rested in its dealings with other nations for many years. In the case of China they were invoked to save a situation which not only threatened the future development and sovereignty of that great Asiatic people, but also threatened to create dangerous and constantly increasing rivalries between the other nations of the world. War had already taken place between Japan and China. At the close of that war three other nations intervened to prevent Japan from obtaining some of the results of that war claimed by her. Other nations sought and had obtained spheres of interest. Partly as a result of these actions a serious uprising had broken out in China which endangered the legations of all of the powers at Peking. While the attack on these legations was in progress, Mr. Hay made an announcement in respect to this policy as the principle upon which the powers should act in the settlement of the rebellion. He said

> The policy of the government of the United States is to seek a solution which may bring about permanent safety and peace to China, preserve Chinese territorial and administrative entity, protect all rights guaranteed to friendly powers by treaty and international law, and safeguard for the world the principle of equal and impartial trade with all parts of the Chinese Empire.

He was successful in obtaining the assent of the other powers to the policy thus announced.

In taking these steps Mr. Hay acted with the cordial support of the British Government. In responding to Mr. Hay's announcement, above set forth, Lord Salisbury, the British Prime Minister expressed himself 'most emphatically as concurring in the policy of the United States'.

For twenty years thereafter the Open Door policy rested upon the informal commitments thus made by the various powers. But in the winter of 1921 to 1922, at a conference participated in by all of the principal powers which had interests in the Pacific, the policy was crystallized into the so-called Nine Power Treaty, which gave definition and precision to the principles upon which the policy rested. In the first article of that Treaty, the contracting powers, other than China, agreed

(1) To respect the sovereignty, the independence and the territorial and administrative integrity of China.

(2) To provide the fullest and most unembarrassed opportunity to China to develop and maintain for herself an effective and stable government.

(3) To use their influence for the purpose of effectually establishing and maintaining the principle of equal opportunity for the commerce and industry of all nations throughout the territory of China.

(4) To refrain from taking advantage of conditions in China in order to seek special rights or privileges which would abridge the rights of subjects or citizens of friendly states, and from countenancing action inimical to the security of such states.

This Treaty thus represents a carefully developed and matured international policy intended, on the one hand, to assure to all of the contracting parties their rights and interests in and with regard to China, and on the other hand, to assure to the people of China the fullest opportunity to develop without molestation their sovereignty and independence according to the modern and enlightened standards believed to maintain among the peoples of this earth. At the time this Treaty was signed, it was known that China was engaged in an attempt to develop the free institutions of a self-governing republic after her recent revolution from an autocratic form of government; that she would require many years of both economic and political effort to that end; and that her progress would necessarily be slow. The Treaty was thus a covenant of self-denial among the signatory powers in deliberate renunciation of any policy of aggression which might tend to interfere with that development. It was believed – and the whole history of the development of the 'Open Door' policy reveals that faith – that only by such a process, under the protection of such an agreement, could the fullest interests not only of China but of all nations which have intercourse with her best be served.

In its report to the President announcing this Treaty, the American Delegation, headed by the then Secretary of State, Mr. Charles E. Hughes, said

It is believed that through this Treaty the 'Open Door' in China has at last been made a fact.

During the course of the discussions which resulted in the Treaty, the Chairman of the British delegation, Lord Balfour, had stated that:

The British Empire delegation understood that there was no representative of any power around the table who thought that the old practice of 'spheres of interest' was either advocated by any government or would be tolerable to this conference. So far as the British Government were concerned, they had, in the most formal manner, publicly announced that they regarded this practice as utterly inappropriate to the existing situation.

At the same time the representative of Japan, Baron Shidehara, announced the position of his Government as follows:

No one denies to China her sacred right to govern herself. No one stands in the way of China to work out her own great national destiny.

The Treaty was originally executed by the United States, Belgium, the British Empire, China, France, Italy, Japan, the Netherlands and Portugal. Subsequently it was also executed by Norway, Bolivia, Sweden, Denmark and Mexico. Germany has signed it but her parliament has not yet ratified it.

It must be remembered also that this Treaty was one of several treaties and agreements entered into at the Washington Conference by the various powers concerned, all of which were interrelated and interdependent. No one of these treaties can be disregarded without disturbing the general understanding and equilibrium which were intended to be accomplished and effected by the group of agreements arrived at in their entirety. The Washington Conference was essentially a disarmament conference, aimed to promote the possibility of peace in the world not only through the cessation of competition in naval armament but also by the solution of various other disturbing problems which threatened the peace of the world, particularly in the Far East. These problems were all interrelated. The willingness of the American Government to surrender its then commanding lead in battleship construction and to leave its positions at Guam and in the Philippines without further fortification, was predicted upon, among other things, the self-denying covenants contained in the Nine Power Treaty, which assured the nations of the world not only of equal opportunity for their Eastern trade but also against the military aggrandizement of any other power at the expense of China. One cannot discuss the possibility of modifying or abrogating those provisions of the Nine Power Treaty without considering at the same time the other promises upon which they were really dependent.

Six years later the policy of self-denial against aggression by a stronger against a weaker power, upon which the Nine Power Treaty had been based, received a powerful reinforcement by the execution by substantially all the nations of the world of the Pact of Paris, the so-called Kellogg-Briand Pact. These two treaties represent independent but harmonious steps taken for the purpose of aligning the conscience and public opinion of the world in favor of a system of orderly development by the law of nations including the settlement of all controversies by methods of justice and peace instead of by arbitrary force. The program for the protection of China from outside aggression is an essential part of any such development. The signatories and adherents of the Nine Power Treaty rightly felt that the orderly and peaceful development of the 400,000,000 of people inhabiting China was necessary to the peaceful welfare of the entire world and that no program for the welfare of the world as a whole could afford to neglect the welfare and protection of China.

The recent events which have taken place in China, especially the hostilities which having been begun in Manchuria have latterly been extended to Shanghai, far from indicating the advisability of any modification of the treaties we have been discussing, have tended to bring home the vital importance of the faithful observance of the covenants therein to all of the nations interested in the Far East. It is not necessary in that connection to inquire into the causes of the controversy or attempt to apportion the blame between the two nations which are unhappily involved; for regardless of cause or responsibility, it is clear beyond peradventure that a situation has developed which cannot, under any circumstances, be reconciled with the obligations of the covenants of these two treaties, and that if the treaties had been faithfully observed such a situation could not have arisen. The signatories of the Nine Power Treaty and of the Kellogg-Briand Pact who are not parties to that conflict are not likely to see any reason for modifying the terms of those treaties. To them the real value of the faithful performance of the treaties has been brought sharply home by the perils and losses to which their nationals have been subjected in Shanghai.

That is the view of this Government. We see no reason for abandoning the enlightened principles which are embodied in these treaties. We believe that this situation would have been avoided had these covenants been faithfully observed, and no evidence has come to us to indicate that a due compliance with them would have interfered with the adequate protection of the legitimate rights in China of the signatories of those treaties and their nationals.

On January 7th last, upon the instruction of the President, this Government formally notified Japan and China that it would not recognize any situation, treaty or agreement entered into by those governments in violation of the covenants of these treaties, which affected the rights of our Government or its citizens in China. If a similar decision should be reached and a similar position taken by the other governments of the world, a caveat will be placed upon such action which, we believe, will effectively bar the legality hereafter of any title or right sought to be obtained by pressure or treaty violation, and which, as has been shown by history in the past, will eventually lead to the restoration to China of rights and titles of which she may have been deprived.

In the past our Government, as one of the leading powers on the Pacific Ocean, has rested its policy upon an abiding faith in the future of the people of China and upon the ultimate success in dealing with them of the principles of fair play, patience, and mutual goodwill. We appreciate the immensity of the task which lies before her statesmen in the development of her country and its government. The delays in her progress, the instability of her attempts to secure a responsible government, were foreseen by Messrs. Hay and Hughes and their contemporaries and were the very obstacles which the policy of the Open Door was designed to meet. We concur with those statesmen, representing all the nations, in the Washington Conference who decided that China was entitled to the time necessary to accomplish her development. We are prepared to make that our policy for the future.

Department of State, *Peace and War: U.S. Foreign Policy, 1931–1941* (Washington, 1943), pp. 168-73. (Hereafter cited as *Peace and War*)

2 'The Quarantine Speech'

Address by President Franklin D. Roosevelt, Chicago, Illinois, October 5, 1937

I am glad to come once again to Chicago and especially to have the opportunity of taking part in the dedication of this important project of civic betterment. . . .

And yet, as I have seen with my own eyes, the prosperous farms, the thriving factories, and the busy railroads – as I have seen the happiness and security and peace which covers our wide land – almost inevitably I have been compelled to contrast our peace with very different scenes being enacted in other parts of the world.

It is because the people of the United States under modern conditions must, for the sake of their own future, give thought to the rest of the world, that I, as the responsible executive head of the Nation, have chosen this great inland city and this gala occasion to speak to you on a subject of definite national importance.

The political situation in the world, which of late has been growing progressively worse, is such as to cause grave concern and anxiety to all the peoples and nations who wish to live in peace and amity with their neighbors. . . .

Without a declaration of war and without warning or justification of any kind, civilians, including women and children, are being ruthlessly murdered with bombs from the air. In times of so-called peace ships are being attacked and sunk by submarines without cause or notice. Nations are fomenting and taking sides in civil warfare in nations that have never done them any harm. Nations claiming freedom for themselves deny it to others.

Innocent peoples and nations are being cruelly sacrificed to a greed for power and supremacy which is devoid of all sense of justice and humane consideration. . . .

If those things come to pass in other parts of the world let no one imagine that America will escape, that it may expect mercy, that the Western Hemisphere will not be attacked, and that it will continue tranquilly and peacefully to carry on the ethics and the arts of civilization.

If those days come 'there will be no safety by arms, no help from authority, no answer in science. The storm will rage till every flower of culture is trampled and all human beings are leveled in a vast chaos.'

If those days are not to come to pass – if we are to have a world in which we can breathe freely and live in amity without fear – the peace-loving nations must make a concerted effort to uphold laws and principles on which alone peace can rest secure.

The peace-loving nations must make a concerted effort in opposition to those violations of treaties and those ignorings of humane instincts which today are creating a state of international anarchy and instability from which there is no escape through mere isolation or neutrality.

Those who cherish their freedom and recognize and respect the equal right of their neighbors to be free and live in peace, must work together for the triumph of law and moral principles in order that peace, justice, and confidence may prevail in the world. There must be a return to a belief in the pledged word, in the value of a signed treaty. There must be recognition of the fact that national morality is as vital as private morality. . . .

There is a solidarity and interdependence about the modern world, both technically and morally, which makes it impossible for any nation completely to isolate itself from economic and political upheavals in the rest of the world, especially when such upheavals appear to be spreading and not declining. There can be no stability or peace either within nations or between nations except under laws and moral standards adhered to by all. International anarchy destroys every foundation for peace. It jeopardizes either the immediate or the future security of every nation, large or small. It is, therefore, a matter of vital interest and concern to the people of the United States that the sanctity of international treaties and the maintenance of international morality be restored. . . .

The situation is definitely of universal concern. The questions involved relate not merely to violations of specific provisions of particular treaties; they are questions of war and of peace, of international law, and especially of principles of humanity. It is true that they involve definite violations of agreements, and especially of the Covenant of the League of Nations, the Briand-Kellogg Pact, and the Nine Power Treaty. But they also involve problems of world economy, world security, and world humanity.

It is true that the moral consciousness of the world must recognize the importance of removing injustices and well-founded grievances; but at the same time it must be aroused to the cardinal necessity of honoring sanctity of treaties, of respecting the rights and liberties of others, and of putting an end to acts of international aggression.

It seems to be unfortunately true that the epidemic of world lawlessness is spreading.

When an epidemic of physical disease starts to spread, the community approves and joins in a quarantine of the patients in order to protect the health of the community against the spread of the disease.

It is my determination to pursue a policy of peace and to adopt every practicable measure to avoid involvement in war. It ought to be inconceivable that in this modern era, and in the face of experience, any nation could be so foolish and ruthless as to run the risk of plunging the whole world into war by invading and violating in contravention of solemn treaties the territory of other nations that have done them no real harm and which are too weak to protect themselves adequately. Yet the peace of the world and the welfare and security of every nation is today being threatened by that very thing.

No nation which refuses to exercise forbearance and to respect the freedom and rights of others can long remain strong and retain the confidence and respect of other nations. No nation ever loses its dignity or good standing by conciliating its differences and by exercising great patience with and consideration for the rights of other nations.

War is a contagion, whether it be declared or undeclared. It can engulf states and peoples remote from the original scene of hostilities. We are determined to keep out of war, yet we cannot insure ourselves against the disastrous effects of war and the dangers of involvement. We are adopting such measures as will minimize our risk of involvement, but we cannot have complete protection in a world of disorder in which confidence and security have broken down.

If civilization is to survive the principles of the Prince of Peace must be restored. Shattered trust between nations must be revived.

Most important of all, the will for peace on the part of peace-loving nations must express itself to the end that nations that may be tempted to violate their agreements and the rights of others will desist from such a cause. There must be positive endeavors to preserve peace.

America hates war. America hopes for peace. Therefore, America actively engages in the search for peace.

Peace and War, pp. 383-7 (excerpts)

3 American Policy at Brussels

Instructions given to Norman Davis, the American delegate to the Brussels Conference, by Secretary Hull, October 18, 1937

A conference having been called of the parties signatory to the Nine Power Treaty signed at Washington February 6, 1922, and the Government of the United States having received and accepted an invitation to participate in this conference, you are to represent the United States.

You will recall that the invitation extended to this Government by the Belgian Government states that the purpose of the conference is 'to examine the situation in the Far East and to study peaceable means of hastening the end of the regrettable conflict which prevails there'....

You will have constantly in mind the character and scope of this country's interest in peace in the Pacific and the Far East as evidenced by the Washington Conference treaties, and especially the rights and interests of the United States under the Nine Power Treaty; the substance and purport of the statement of this Government's position made by the Secretary of State on October 6; also statements relating to foreign policy made by the President in his address at Chicago on October 5 and in his broadcast from Washington on October 12. You will bear in mind that the first objective of the foreign policy of this country is national security, and that consequently we seek to keep peace and to promote the maintenance of peace; that we believe in cooperative effort for the preservation of peace by pacific and practicable means; and that this country has as a signatory of the Pact of Paris of 1928 renounced war as an instrument of national policy and pledged itself to resort for settlement of disputes to none but pacific means. You will bear in mind also that public opinion in the United States has expressed its emphatic determination that the United States keep out of war.

It is the hope of this Government that this conference may be able to achieve results which will contribute toward permanent stability and peace in the Far East. In the concept of this Government, the primary function of the conference is to provide a forum for constructive discussion, to formulate and suggest possible bases of settlement, and to endeavor to bring the parties together through peaceful negotiation.

Peace and War, pp. 389-90

4 'The Green Light Message'

Ambassador Joseph Grew to Secretary of State Cordell Hull, September 12, 1940

The observations of Mr. A. T. Steele concerning Japan, recently received here by mail, have had my careful attention. In general terms I believe that Mr. Steele's observations are well-founded and sound, a belief which applies equally to the important considerations advanced in the final two paragraphs of the summary of Mr. Steele's statement.

His thesis that 'firmness is the soundest and safest American naval policy' and that 'the risks involved are much less than is commonly supposed in the United States' is however of such far-reaching gravity as to deserve carefully studied analysis and comment. In presenting the present trend of my thoughts on this general subject I have constantly in mind the fact that the shaping of our policy vis-à-vis Japan must depend upon the broader viewpoint of the Administration in Washington and upon many factors which may not be apparent to this Embassy. . . .

Whatever may be the intentions of the present Japanese Government, there can be no doubt that the army and other elements in the country see in the present world situation a 'golden opportunity' to carry into effect their dreams of expansion; the German victories have gone to their heads like strong wine; until recently they have believed implicitly in the defeat of Great Britain; they have argued that the war will probably end in a quick German victory and that it is well to consolidate Japan's position in greater East Asia while Germany is still acquiescent and before the eventual hypothetical strengthening of German naval power might rob Japan of far flung control in the Far East; they have discounted effective opposition on the part of the United States although carefully watching our attitude. The ability of the saner heads in and out of the Government to control those elements has been and is doubtful.

Now, however, I sense a gradual change in the outburst of exhilaration which greeted the new Government on its inception. The Japanese Government, the army and navy and the public are beginning to see that Germany may not defeat Great Britain after all, a hypothesis which I have constantly emphasized to my Japanese contacts in the plainest language and now to add to that dawning realization, they see the United States and Great Britain steadily drawing closer together in measures of mutual defense with the American acquisition of naval bases in British possessions in the Atlantic and with our support of the British fleet by the transfer of fifty destroyers. They hear reports of our haste to build a two-ocean navy and of our considering the strengthening of our naval bases in the Pacific and even rumors of our eventual use of Singapore. These developments and rumors are having their logical effect on Japanese consciousness. On the one hand they tend to emphasize the potential danger which Japan faces from eventual positive action by the United States and Great Britain acting together (the danger of combined Anglo-American measures has long been appreciated in Japan as evidenced by efforts to avoid irritating the

United States and Great Britain simultaneously) or by the United States alone. On the other hand they furnish cogent arguments for those elements in Japan who seek economic and political security by obtaining markets and sources of raw materials wholly within the control of Japan. As for Germany, the Japanese are beginning to question whether even a victorious Germany would not provide a new hazard to their expansionist program both in China and in the southward advance. Meanwhile the future position and attitude of Soviet Russia is always an uncertain factor in their calculations. These various considerations are beginning to give them concern.

High-pressure diplomacy, especially in the Netherlands East Indies, will continue, but the fact that the Japanese Government was able even temporarily to restrain the military forces from their plans for a headlong invasion of Indochina indicates a degree of caution which I do not doubt was at least partially influenced by the attitude of the United States. What Mr. Steele describes as the 'nibbling policy' appears likely to continue until the world situation, and especially the attitude of the United States, becomes clearer.

In previous communications I have expressed the opinion that sanctions by the United States would set Japanese-American relations on a downward curve. It is true that our own newly instituted program of national preparedness now justifies measures which need not fall within the realm of outright sanctions. On the other hand we must envisage the probability that drastic embargoes on the export of such important products as petroleum, of which the United States is known to possess a superabundance would be interpreted by the Japanese Government and people as actually sanctions which might and probably would lead to some form of retaliation. The risks which Mr. Steele sees as 'much less than is commonly supposed in the United States' will depend less upon the careful calculations of the Japanese Government than upon the uncalculated 'do or die' temper of the Army and Navy in case they should attribute to the United States the responsibility for the failure of their expansionist plans. Such retaliation might take the form of countermeasures by the Government but there would be even greater likelihood of some sudden stroke by the army or navy without the Government's prior knowledge or authorization. These risks constitute an imponderable factor which cannot at any given moment be weighed with assurance. It would be shortsighted, however, to deny their existence or to proceed with the formulation of policy and the adoption of measures without giving these potential risks full consideration and determining the wisdom of squarely facing these risks.

In the ensuing observations I am carefully considering both of the fundamental purposes of my mission, namely the protection and advancement of American interests and the maintenance of good relations between the United States and Japan. When these two desiderata conflict, the preponderant emphasis to be placed on the one or the other is a matter of high policy which does not lie within my competency. My object is merely to place before the Administration in Washington the outstanding factors in the situation as we see them from the angle of this Embassy. Having carefully set forth the inevitable hazards involved in a strong policy I now respectfully turn to the hazards involved in a laissez-faire policy.

In discussing the specific question of American-Japanese relations it is impossible to view that problem in its proper perspective without considering it as part and parcel of the world problem which, briefly, presents the following aspects:

> The United States and Great Britain are the leaders of a great group of English speaking nations around the world standing for a 'way of life' which is being appallingly threatened today by a group of Germany, Italy, Soviet Russia and Japan whose avowed purpose is to impose by force of arms their will upon conquered peoples. In attempting to deal with such powers the uses of diplomacy are in general bankrupt.
>
> Diplomacy may occasionally retard but cannot effectively stem the tide. Force or the display of force can alone prevent these powers from attaining their objectives. Japan today is one of the predatory powers; she has submerged all moral and ethical sense and has become frankly and unashamedly opportunist, seeking at every turn to profit by the weakness of others. Her policy of southward expansion is a definite threat to American interests in the Pacific and is a thrust at the British Empire in the East.
>
> American security has admittedly depended in a measure upon the existence of the British fleet which in turn has been, and could only have been, supported by the British Empire.
>
> If we conceive it to be in our interest to support the British Empire in this hour of her travail, and I most emphatically do so conceive it, we must strive by every means to preserve the status quo in the Pacific at least until the European war has been won or lost. In my opinion this cannot be done nor can our interests be further adequately and properly protected by merely registering disapproval and keeping a careful record thereof. It is clear that Japan has been

deterred from taking greater liberties with American interests only out of respect for our potential power; it is equally clear that she has trampled upon our rights to a degree in precise ratio to the strength of her conviction that the American people would not permit that power to be used. Once that conviction is shaken it is possible that the uses of diplomacy may again become accepted.

If then we can by firmness preserve the status quo in the Pacific until and if Britain emerges successfully from the European struggle, Japan will be faced with a situation which will make it impossible for the present opportunist philosophy to maintain the upper hand. At a moment it might then be possible to undertake a readjustment of the whole Pacific problem on a fair, frank, and equitable basis to the lasting benefit of both the United States and of Japan. Until such time as there is a complete regeneration of thought in this country, a show of force, together with a determination to employ it if need be, can alone contribute effectively to the achievement of such an outcome and to our own future security.

Passing from the general to the specific problem that now confronts us, and with the foregoing picture in mind, I applauded the timeliness of the instructions from the Department concerning the Shanghai defense sectors. The Department will have seen from my report of September 4 that the Foreign Minister's complaint as to alleged threats on our part was met with the statement that what we have in mind is 'a logical reciprocal adjustment of international relations.' I feel that the appropriate time has come to proceed, gradually but progressively with that adjustment. In the present situation and outlook I believe that the time has come when continued patience and restraint on the part of the United States may and probably will lead to developments which will render Japanese-American relations progressively precarious. It is my hope that if the Japanese Government and people can be led to believe that their hand is being overplayed, there will eventually ensue a reverse swing of the pendulum in which a reconstruction of good relations between the United States and Japan will be possible. The alternative seems to me to be hopeless.

The foregoing analysis, which has been drafted with care over a period of several days, has the expressed complete concurrence of the Naval, Military and Commercial Attachés and all other members of the immediate staff of this Embassy.

Papers Relating to the Foreign Relations of the United States, Vol. IV (Washington, 1955 *1940*), pp. 599-603.

5 Embargo against Japan

(a) *Memorandum by Acting Secretary of State Sumner Welles of a conversation between President Roosevelt and the Japanese Ambassador, July 24, 1941*

At the request of the Japanese Ambassador, the President received the Ambassador for an off-the-record conference in the Oval Room at the White House at five o'clock this afternoon. At the President's request, Admiral Stark and I were present.

At the outset of the conference the President made approximately the following statement to the Ambassador. The President said, referring to a talk which he had made this morning to a home defense group under the leadership of Mayor LaGuardia, that for more than two years the United States had been permitting oil to be exported from the United States to Japan. He said that this had been done because of the realization on the part of the United States that if these oil supplies had been shut off or restricted the Japanese Government and people would have been furnished with an incentive or a pretext for moving down upon the Netherlands East Indies in order to assure themselves of a greater oil supply than that which, under present conditions, they were able to obtain. The United States had been pursuing this policy primarily for the purpose of doing its utmost to play its full part in making the effort to preserve peace in the Pacific region. At the present time, the President said, the Ambassador undoubtedly knew that there was a very considerable shortage in the oil supply in the eastern part of the United States and the average American man and woman were unable to understand why, at a time when they themselves were asked to curtail their use of gasoline oil, the United States Government should be permitting oil supplies to continue to be exported to Japan when Japan during these past two years had given every indication of pursuing a policy of force and conquest in conjunction with the policy of world conquest and domination which Hitler was carrying on. The average American citizen could not understand why his Government was permitting Japan to be furnished with oil in order that such oil might be utilized by Japan in carrying on her purposes of aggression. The President said that if Japan attempted to seize oil supplies by force in the Netherlands East Indies, the Dutch would, without the shadow of a doubt, resist, the British would immediately come to their assistance, war would then result between Japan, the British and the Dutch, and, in view of our own policy of assisting

Great Britain, an exceedingly serious situation would immediately result. It was with all of these facts in mind, the President said, that notwithstanding the bitter criticism that had been leveled against the Administration and against the Department of State, the President up to now had permitted oil to be shipped by Japan from the United States.

The President then went on to say that this new move by Japan in Indochina created an exceedingly serious problem for the United States. He said that, as I had stated to the Ambassador yesterday, insofar as assuring itself that it could obtain foodstuffs and raw materials from Indochina, Japan, of course, had it reached an agreement with the United States along the terms of the discussions between Secretary Hull and the Ambassador, would have been afforded far greater assurances of obtaining such supplies on equal terms with any other nation. More than that, the President said, the cost of any military occupation is tremendous and the occupation itself is not conducive to the production by civilians in occupied countries of food supplies and raw materials of the character required by Japan. Had Japan undertaken to obtain the supplies she required from Indochina in a peaceful way, she not only would have obtained larger quantities of such supplies, but would have obtained them with complete security and without the draining expense of a military occupation. Furthermore, from the military standpoint, the President said, surely the Japanese Government could not have in reality the slightest belief that China, Great Britain, the Netherlands or the United States had any territorial designs on Indochina nor were in the slightest degree providing any real threats of aggression against Japan. This Government, consequently, could only assume that the occupation of Indochina was being undertaken by Japan for the purpose of further offense and this created a situation which necessarily must give the United States the most serious disquiet.

The President said that he had been following in complete detail the conversations which had been progressing between Secretary Hull and the Ambassador and that he was confident that the Ambassador would agree that the policies now undertaken in Indochina by the Japanese Government were completely opposed to the principles and the letter of the proposed agreement which had been under discussion. . . .

The President then said that he had a proposal to make to the Ambassador which had occurred to him just before the Ambassador had come in and which he had not had time to talk over with me before making his proposal to the Ambassador.

The President said that it might be too late for him to make this proposal but he felt that no matter how late the hour might be, he still wished to seize every possible opportunity of preventing the creation of a situation between Japan and the United States which could only give rise to serious misunderstandings between the two peoples. The President stated that if the Japanese Government would refrain from occupying Indochina with its military and naval forces, or, had such steps actually been commenced, if the Japanese Government would withdraw such forces, the President could assure the Japanese Government that he would do everything within his power to obtain from the Governments of China, Great Britain, the Netherlands, and of course the United States itself a binding and solemn declaration, provided Japan would undertake the same commitment, to regard Indochina as a neutralized country in the same way in which Switzerland had up to now been regarded by the powers as a neutralized country. He stated that this would imply that none of the powers concerned would undertake any military act of aggression against Indochina and would refrain from the exercise of any military control within or over Indochina. He would further endeavor to procure from Great Britain and the other pertinent powers a guarantee that so long as the present emergency continued, the local French authorities in Indochina would remain in control of the territory and would not be confronted with attempts to dislodge them on the part of de Gaullist or Free French agents or forces.

If these steps were taken, the President said, Japan would be given solemn and binding proof that no other power had any hostile designs upon Indochina and that Japan would be afforded the fullest and freest opportunity of assuring herself of the source of food supplies and other raw materials in Indochina which she was seeking to secure.

The Ambassador then reiterated concisely and quite clearly what the President had suggested. He then made some statement which was not quite clear to the effect that such a step would be very difficult at this time on account of the face-saving element involved on the part of Japan and that only a very great statesman would reverse a policy at this time. . . .

(b) *Statement issued by the White House, July 26, 1941*

In view of the unlimited national emergency declared by the President, he issued, on July 26, an Executive order freezing Japanese assets in the United States in the same manner in which assets of various European countries were frozen on June 14, 1941. This measure, in effect, brings all financial and import and export trade transactions in which Japanese interests are involved under the control of the Government and imposes criminal penalties for violation of the order.

This Executive order, just as the order of June 14, 1941, is designed among other things to prevent the use of the financial facilities of the United States and trade between Japan and the United States in ways harmful to national defense and American interests, to prevent the liquidation in the United States of assets obtained by duress or conquest, and to curb subversive activities in the United States.

At the specific request of Generalissimo Chiang Kai-shek, and for the purpose of helping the Chinese Government, the President has, at the same time, extended the freezing control to Chinese assets in the United States. The administration of the licensing system with respect to Chinese assets will be conducted with a view to strengthening the foreign trade and exchange position of the Chinese Government. The inclusion of China in the Executive Order, in accordance with the wishes of the Chinese Government, is a continuation of this Government's policy of assisting China.

Peace and War, pp. 699-705

6 The Final Proposals before Pearl Harbor

(a) *The Japanese Proposal of November 20, 1941, given by Ambassador Nomura to Secretary Hull*

(1) Both the Governments of Japan and the United States undertake not to make any armed advancement into any of the regions in the South-eastern Asia and the Southern Pacific area excepting the part of French Indo-China where the Japanese troops are stationed at present.

(2) The Japanese Government undertakes to withdraw its troops now stationed in French Indo-China upon either the restoration of peace between Japan and China or the establishment of an equitable peace in the Pacific area.

In the meantime the Government of Japan declares that it is prepared to remove its troops now stationed in the southern part of French Indo-China to the northern part of the said territory upon the conclusion of the present arrangement which shall later be embodied in the final agreement.

(3) The Government of Japan and the United States shall cooperate with a view to securing the acquisition of those goods and commodities which the two countries need in Netherlands East Indies.

(4) The Governments of Japan and the United States mutually undertake to restore their commercial relations to those prevailing prior to the freezing of the assets.

The Government of the United States shall supply Japan a required quantity of oil.

(5) The Government of the United States undertakes to refrain from such measures and actions as will be prejudicial to the endeavors for the restoration of general peace between Japan and China.

(b) *The American Counter-Proposal of November 26, 1941 given by Secretary Hull to Ambassador Nomura*

OUTLINE OF PROPOSED BASIS FOR AGREEMENT BETWEEN THE UNITED STATES AND JAPAN

SECTION I

Draft Mutual Declaration of Policy

The Government of the United States and the Government of Japan both being solicitous for the peace of the Pacific affirm that their national policies are directed toward lasting and extensive peace throughout the Pacific area, that they have no territorial designs in that area, that they have no intention of threatening other countries or of using military force aggressively against any neighboring nation and that, accordingly, in their national policies they will actively support and give practical application to the following fundamental principles upon which their relations with each other and with all other governments are based:

(1) The principle of inviolability of territorial integrity and sovereignty of each and all nations.

(2) The principle of non-interference in the internal affairs of other countries.

(3) The principle of equality, including equality of commercial opportunity and treatment.

(4) The principle of reliance upon international cooperation and conciliation for the prevention and pacific settlement of controversies and for improvement of international conditions by peaceful methods and processes.

The Government of Japan and the Government of the United States have agreed that toward eliminating chronic political instability, preventing recurrent economic collapse, and providing a basis for peace, they will actively support and practically apply the following principles in their economic relations with each other and with other nations and peoples:

(1) The principle of non-discrimination in international commercial relations.

(2) The principle of international economic cooperation and abolition of extreme nationalism as expressed in excessive trade restrictions.

(3) The principle of non-discriminatory access by all nations to raw material supplies.

(4) The principle of full protection of the interests of consuming countries and populations as regards the operation of international commodity agreements.

(5) The principle of establishment of such institutions and arrangements of international finance as may lend aid to the essential enterprises and the continuous development of all countries and may permit payments through processes of trade consonant with the welfare of all countries.

SECTION II

Steps to be taken by the Government of the United States and by the Government of Japan

The Government of the United States and the Government of Japan propose to take steps as follows:

(1) The Government of the United States and the Government of Japan will endeavor to conclude a multilateral non-aggression pact among the British Empire, China, Japan, the Netherlands, the Soviet Union, Thailand and the United States.

(2) Both Governments will endeavor to conclude among the American, British, Chinese, Japanese, the Netherland and Thai Governments an agreement whereunder each of the Governments would pledge itself to respect the territorial integrity of French Indochina and, in the event that there should develop a threat to the territorial integrity of Indochina, to enter into immediate consultation with a view to taking such measures as may be deemed necessary and advisable to meet the threat in question. Such agreement would provide also that each of the Governments party to the agreement would not seek or accept preferential treatment in its trade or economic relations with Indochina and would use its influence to obtain for each of the signatories equality of treatment in trade and commerce with French Indochina.

(3) The Government of Japan will withdraw all military, naval, air and police forces from China and from Indochina.

(4) The Government of the United States and the Government of Japan will not support – militarily, politically, economically – any government or regime in China other than the National Government of the Republic of China with capital temporarily at Chungking.

(5) Both Governments will give up all extraterritorial rights in China, including rights and interests in and with regard to international settlements and concessions, and rights under the Boxer Protocol of 1901.

Both Governments will endeavor to obtain the agreement of the British and other governments to give up extraterritorial rights in China, including rights in international settlements and in concessions and under the Boxer Protocol of 1901.

(6) The Government of the United States and the Government of Japan will enter into negotiations for the conclusion between the United States and Japan of a trade agreement, based upon reciprocal most-favored-nation treatment and reduction of trade barriers by both countries, including an undertaking by the United States to bind raw silk on the free list.

(7) The Government of the United States and the Government of Japan will, respectively, remove the freezing restrictions on Japanese funds in the United States and on American funds in Japan.

(8) Both Governments will agree upon a plan for the stabilization of the dollar-yen rate, with the allocation of funds adequate for this purpose, half to be supplied by Japan and half by the United States.

(9) Both Governments will agree that no agreement which either has concluded with any third power or powers shall be interpreted by it in such a way as to conflict with the fundamental purpose of this agreement, the establishment and preservation of peace throughout the Pacific area.

(10) Both Governments will use their influence to cause other governments to adhere to and to give practical application to the basic political and economic principles set forth in this agreement.

Peace and War, pp. 800–801, 810–12

IV

THE NEW DEAL FROM ISOLATION TO WAR

The policies of the Roosevelt administration toward the gathering storm in Europe evolved with painful slowness. America was little more than a bystander until the twin shocks of Dunkirk and the French collapse of 1940 galvanised the United States into an active policy.

Throughout his first term in office (1933–37), and for quite some time afterwards, President Roosevelt focused his attention almost exclusively upon domestic concerns, and foreign policy was often sacrificed on the altar of New Deal reforms. FDR was never willing to adopt any diplomatic stance which might threaten the fulfilment of his domestic programme. At the very outset of his administration his attitude toward the London Economic Conference revealed the fact that his foreign policy was shaped and guided by strictly domestic criteria. His message of July 2, 1933 so effectively torpedoed that international gathering that it almost immediately sank without trace (1). There were those – John Maynard Keynes was one – who agreed with Roosevelt's criticism and who believed that the London Conference was pursuing outmoded, irrelevant economic objectives. Nevertheless, the London Conference marked the last time that the nations of the world attempted to deal with the depression through international action; Roosevelt's crushing veto underlined the fact that the United States, in company with many other countries, was about to become inner-directed. But Secretary of State Cordell Hull, building on the foundation laid by his Republican predecessors, did outline the Good Neighbor policy in inter-American relations at the Pan American Conference held at Montevideo in December 1933. His willingness to sign the Argentine anti-war pact – as well as several other Latin-sponsored resolutions on the rights and duties of states – indicated that the United States was now formally willing to renounce unilateral intervention in both principle and practice (2).

It is entirely correct to emphasise the fact of American isolationism in the 1930s – indeed, to describe it as a veritable 'blizzard' of isolationism. The overriding effect of the depression was to turn the American mind inwards to domestic problems. Increasing signs of the approaching collapse of the European order simply led Congress to conclude that the United States must, no matter what the cost, insulate itself from any and all conflicts. Senator Gerald Nye's well publicised investigation of the munitions industry persuaded thousands of Americans that an unholy alliance of bankers and munitions makers – the notorious 'merchants of death' – had deliberately manœuvred America into war in 1917 for no more honourable motive than the desire for profits (**3** (**a**)). Congress, convinced that it was directly applying the lessons of history, responded between 1935 and 1937 by passing a series of so-called Neutrality Laws designed to prevent any recurrence of the experience of 1917. If war broke out anywhere in the world, Americans could not trade with the belligerents, send their ships into war zones, travel on belligerent ships, or lend money to those at war. It was believed that America would be securely isolated from war behind this legislative Maginot Line (**3** (**b**)).

President Roosevelt, though clearly unhappy about the restrictions which the Neutrality Laws imposed upon his freedom of action, reluctantly signed them. But FDR, still giving priority to domestic issues, chafed only to himself, and in his campaign for re-election to a second term, exhibited a willingness to float along with the high tide of isolationism. In a campaign speech at Chautauqua, New York, in August 1936, he identified himself and his party with those who wished to insulate America from all conflict (**4**).

In 1937 and 1938 Roosevelt and Hull showed clear signs of increasing concern about the international situation. The President long toyed with the idea of holding a great international conference in Washington to seek solutions to the issues causing conflict. Still, whenever Hull spoke about growing international tensions and attempted to define American foreign policy, he confined his remarks to moralistic pronouncements of general principles and offered nothing more concrete than broad and cautious generalities about the 'need to avoid the extremes either of internationalism or of isolationism' (**5**). Moreover, as late as Munich – at the hour of Europe's gravest crisis since Sarajevo – the United States remained a bystander and 'the eternal question mark'. The President's cable to Adolf Hitler on September 27, 1938, was truly representative of the American position in world affairs; FDR hoped that war could still be avoided, urged the Munich powers to continue their negotiations, but refused to assume any American responsibilities for any agreements that might emerge (**6**). After Chamberlain returned from Munich, Roosevelt sent him a cryptic two-word cable: 'Good man'.

The French collapse in May and June of 1940 brought a still unsuspecting America, lulled into repose during the 'phony war', face to face with the prospect that, should Britain also be defeated, the United States would stand virtually alone in an Axis-dominated world. Roosevelt rejected all pleas that the United States become a belligerent. But, in his speech of June 10, 1940, at the graduation ceremonies of the University of Virginia, he made his 'great commitment'. The Charlottesville speech is usually remembered for its dramatic reference to Mussolini's stab in the back of prostrate France, but its real importance was that, in essence, it laid down the principal lines of policy that the United States was to follow from the summer of 1940 until Pearl Harbor. Implicit in it was the policy of providing all possible American aid to countries fighting Fascism, the policy of 'all aid short of war' (7). Roosevelt's great commitment was both a sign of his faith in Britain's survival and a rare act of political courage. It was made at a time when his campaign for a third term as President – for which there was no precedent in American history – was about to begin and against the advice of his principal advisers who, doubting Britain's ability to resist, urged him to preserve all war materials for America's own defence. In June of 1940 the American army was considerably smaller than the army of Leopold's Belgium which the *Wehrmacht* had just crushed.

The growing Anglo-American partnership and the policy of all aid short of war were furthered in the late summer of 1940 by the arrangement whereby Roosevelt (properly, Roosevelt, for it was a Presidential decision) 'traded' fifty over-age American destroyers for a series of leases on British bases in the Western Hemisphere (**8**). The policy was formalised by the Lend-Lease Act of 1941 (**9**). Ultimately, as the United States became, in Roosevelt's words, 'the great arsenal of democracy', America gradually edged toward an undeclared shooting war in the Atlantic.

Throughout 1941 Roosevelt refused to go beyond the framework of all aid short of war. He moved one step at a time, from one crisis to the next, ever careful not to move beyond what he thought Congress and the American public would accept. Above all he insisted that the United States must not commit the ultimate overt act, must not take the final step from which retreat was impossible. His policy of gradualism was a masterful performance, fully demonstrated by his radio address in September 1941 when an American destroyer, the *Greer*, was sunk in the Atlantic (**10**).

Roosevelt's caution was a compound of many factors. Adolf Hitler, whose own memory encompassed the German blunders of 1917, would never give his submarine commanders full authorisation to sink American vessels. More important, the American public was still bitterly divided on the issue of war or peace; all authorities agree that, at no time before Pearl Harbor, did a majority of the American people believe that the United States should become a belligerent. Even those organised groups which supported the administration never advocated any policy beyond that of all aid short of war. Of decisive influence was the existence, at the other pole of public opinion, of a highly organised and extremely articulate opposition, 'America First'. Those who spoke for America First charged that Europe's war was none of America's business and, at every turn in the road, accused Roosevelt of a deliberate plot to plunge America into the conflict. The article by ex-President Hoover and the speech by Charles A. Lindbergh, once the popular idol of the 1920s, accurately reflect the depth and intensity of the isolationist assault upon Roosevelt (**11 (a)**, **11 (b)**). And, as the excerpts from the memoirs of the Republican Congressional leader, Joe Martin, well indicate, there was always politics, ever a factor in the American system, to consider (**12**). It was because Franklin Roosevelt was the master of this system that, at the time of Pearl Harbor, he had behind him a united and not a divided nation.

I Message from President Roosevelt to the London Economic Conference

July 2, 1933 to Cordell Hull

Herewith is a statement which I think you can use Monday morning as a message from me to you. If you think it best not to give it out in London let me know at once and in that event I will release it here as a White House statement.

'I would regard it as a catastrophe amounting to a world tragedy if the great Conference of Nations, called to bring about a more real and permanent financial stability and a greater prosperity to the masses of all nations, should, in advance of any serious effort to consider these broader problems, allow itself to be diverted by the proposal of a purely artificial and temporary experiment affecting the monetary exchange of a few nations only. Such action, such diversion, shows a singular lack of proportion and a failure to remember the larger purposes for which the Economic Conference originally was called together.

I do not relish the thought that insistence on such action should be made an excuse for the continuance of the basic economic errors that underlie so much of the present world wide depression.

The world will not long be lulled by the specious fallacy of achieving a temporary and probably an artificial stability in foreign exchange on the part of a few large countries only.

The sound internal economic system of a nation is a greater factor in its well being than the price of its currency in changing terms of the currencies of other nations.

It is for this reason that reduced cost of government, adequate government income, and ability to service government debts are all so important to ultimate stability. So too, old fetishes of so-called international bankers are being replaced by efforts to plan national currencies with the objective of giving to those currencies a continuing purchasing power which does not greatly vary in terms of the commodities and need of modern civilization. Let me be frank in saying that the United States seeks the kind of a dollar which a generation hence will have the same purchasing and debt paying power as the dollar value we hope to attain in the near future. That objective means more to the good of other nations than a fixed ratio for a month or two in terms of the pound or franc.

Our broad purpose is the permanent stabilization of every nation's currency. Gold or gold and silver can well continue to be a metallic reserve behind currencies but this is not the time to dissipate gold reserves. When the world works out concerted policies in the majority of nations to produce balanced budgets and living within their means, then we can properly discuss a better distribution of the world's gold and silver supply to act as a reserve base of national currencies. Restoration of world trade is an important partner, both in the means and in the result. Here also temporary exchange fixing is not the true answer. We must rather mitigate existing embargoes to make easier the exchange of products which one nation has and the other nation has not.

The Conference was called to better and perhaps to cure fundamental economic ills. It must not be diverted from that effort.'

Papers relating to the Foreign Relations of the United States, 1933, Vol. I (Washington, 1950), pp. 673–4.

2 Statement by Cordell Hull at the 7th International Conference of American States

Montevideo, December 15, 1933

MR. CHAIRMAN AND MEMBERS OF THE COMMITTEE: I arise to say that the Delegation of the United States of America is in the heartiest accord with the very timely and vitally important resolution offered by the able Minister of Foreign Affairs of Argentina, Dr. Saavedra Lamas. The beneficial benefits of this proposal on peace will be far-reaching. Their stimulating influence will extend beyond this hemisphere and to the uttermost parts of the earth. They will bring cheer and hope to the struggling and discouraged forces of peace everywhere. . . .

I desire most heartily to second the motion to report this resolution favorably. I desire also to say that the United States is ready to affix its signature to the Argentine anti-war pact, and I venture at the same time to express the earnest hope that representatives of all other governments present will aid in a great service to peace by signifying at this time their willingness to affix on behalf of their governments their signatures on any of these five treaties which they have not yet signed. . . .

Peace and economic rehabilitation must be our objective. The avoidance of war must be our supreme purpose. Most gratifying is the practical appeal which your leaders are making to bring about an end to the bloody conflict between two of our sister republics, the one small and remaining exception to our hopes and ideals for enduring peace in this hemisphere. This is a blot on our civilization which we must erase. I grant with all my heart that with the end of that conflict war as an instrument for settling international disputes will have lost its last foothold in this hemisphere.

In its own forward-looking policy the administration at Washington has pledged itself, as I have said, to the policy of the good neighbor. As President Roosevelt has defined the good neighbor, he 'resolutely respects himself and, because he does so, respects the rights of others'. We must think, we must speak, we must act this part.

I am safe in the statement that each of the American nations wholeheartedly supports this doctrine – that every nation alike earnestly favors the absolute independence, the unimpaired sovereignty, the perfect equality, and the political integrity of each nation, large or small, as they similarly oppose aggression in every sense of the word.

May I for a moment direct attention to the significance of this broad policy as my country is steadily carrying it into effect under the Roosevelt administration, the extent and nature of which should be familiar to each of the nations here represented. My Government is doing its utmost, with due regard to commitments made in the past, to end with all possible speed engagements which have been set up by previous circumstances. There are some engagements which can be removed more speedily than others. In some instances disentanglement from obligations of another era can only be brought about through the exercise of some patience. The United States is determined that its new policy of the New Deal – of enlightened liberalism – shall have full effect and shall be recognized in its fullest import by its neighbors. The people of my country strongly feel that the so-called right of conquest must forever be banished from this hemisphere, and most of all they shun and reject that so-called right for themselves. The New Deal indeed would be an empty boast if it did not mean that.

Let us in the broad spirit of this revitalized policy make this the beginning of a great new era, of a great renaissance in American cooperative effort to promote our entire material, moral, and spiritual affairs and to erect an edifice of peace that will forever endure. . .

Peace and War, pp. 195-9 (excerpts)

3 The Search for Neutrality

(a) *The Investigation of the Munitions Industry: Speech in the United States Senate by Senator Gerald P. Nye, May 28, 1935*

. . . This past year has witnessed the most intensive inquiry into the questions of arms traffic, munitions, war profits, and profits from preparedness for war that the world ever saw undertaken. It has been my privilege to work with six other Members of the United States Senate in this study. I am happy tonight to say that it grows increasingly evident that our labors have not been in vain and that truly worth-while legislation will be forthcoming to meet the frightful challenge which the inquiry disclosures have been. Largely because the people have shown tremendous interest in the subject, I am sure that substantial legislation is on the way to restrain those racketeers who find large profit in breeding hate, fear, and suspicion as a base for large preparedness programs, and who have learned that while there is large profit in preparing for war, there is larger profit for them in war itself.

But out of this year of study has come tremendous conviction that our American welfare requires that great importance be given the subject of our neutrality when others are at war.

Tonight I think we will do well to give some thought to causes behind our entry into the Great War. Those causes as well as the results which have since followed are an experience we should not soon forget.

Nineteen hundred and fourteen found America just as determined, just as anxious for peace as it is now. But less than 3 years later we were in the greatest of all wars, creating obligations and burdens which even to this day bend our backs. What was it that took us into that war in spite of our high contrary resolve?

To me there is something sinister involved in using the language of 1914 in this present pre-war year of 1935. There is, I fear, danger that the soft, evasive, unrealistic, untrue language of 21 years ago will again take root and then rise up and slay its millions as it did then, both during and after a war.

Let me make this clear. If the people of the world are told again that the next war is a political war for the noblest possible ideals, those same people will be the ones to suffer not only during the war, but also when the war is over and the peace signed on the basis of the crude, economic struggle.

Did the English or the Germans or the French in 1914 know that they were fighting the battle of commercial rivalries? No. Did the

American people know that they were fighting to save the skins of the bankers who had coaxed the people into loaning $2,000,000,000 to the Allies? No. They all thought that they were fighting for national honor, for democracy, for the end of war. . . .

Let us be as frank before the next war comes as Wilson was frank after the last war was over. Let us know that it is sales and shipments of munitions and contraband, and the lure of the profits in them, that will get us into another war, and that when the proper time comes and we talk about national honor, let us know that simply means the right to go on making money out of a war.

Let us have done with all the fraud, and we will have done with all the post-war friction.

There are many who have tried to keep us from being involved in entangling foreign political alliances. But since wars are for economic causes basically, it is as important to avoid becoming involved in entangling foreign economic alliances. That is the crux of the matter. It is useless to pretend that our isolation from foreign political entanglements means anything if we open wide the gates to foreign loans and credits for munitions and spread out a network of munition ships that will be ignition points of another war.

What are the facts behind these conclusions of men familiar with the real causes of our entering the war?

From the year ending June 30, 1914, to the year ending June 30, 1916, our exports to the Allies increased almost 300 percent, or from $825,000,000 to $3,214,000,000. During the same period our exports to the Central Powers fell from $169,000,000 to $1,000,000. Long before we declared war on Germany we had ceased to have any economic interests in her fate in the war, because she was buying nothing from us.

The bulk of our sales during this pre-war period were in munitions and war materials. It must be remembered that the World War inaugurated war on the scale of whole nations pitted against nations – not simply of armies, however large, against armies. Consequently, foodstuffs and raw materials for the manufacture of items essential to modern war were declared contraband by one belligerent or another. In the year 1914 more than half of our total exports to all countries were munitions and war materials of this kind. In 1915 our sales of such materials were 179 percent greater than they had been in the preceding year and constituted 86 percent of our total exports to all countries. In 1916 our sales of these articles were 287 percent greater than in 1914 and totaled $3,700,000,000, which was 88 percent of our total exports. The growth of our sales of explosives may be taken as a single example. In the year ending June 30, 1914, we exported only $10,000,000 worth of explosives. In the year ending June 30, 1915, this figure had grown to $189,000,000, and in the next year it reached $715,000,000.

America officially regarded the right to engage in this trade as part of our neutral rights and no attempt was made to discourage it. . . .

Now, we must not forget that this enormous trade required financing also on an enormous scale. Our State Department at the outset of the war announced that 'in the judgment of this Government loans by American bankers to any foreign nation which is at war are inconsistent with the true spirit of neutrality.' But once we had recognized and encouraged the trade in war materials as a neutral right, it proved impossible to deny the demands for normal financing of that trade.

While the State Department was officially opposed to loans, our bankers were not. Mr. Lamont has written that J. P. Morgan & Co. was whole-heartedly in back of the Allies from the start. Mr. Davison was sent to England to place the firm's services at England's disposal. As early as February 1915 Morgan signed his first contract with the Du Pont Co. as agent for an allied power. Of the total sales by Du Pont to France and England, totalling practically half a billion dollars, over 70 percent were made through Morgan & Co., although Morgan & Co. acted as agents for the Allies only from the spring of 1915 until shortly after we entered the war – a little over 2 years.

From the early days of the war the State Department did not object to bank credits being extended to belligerents as distinguished from loans. In November 1914 France received $10,000,000 on 1-year treasury notes from the National City Bank, and in May 1915 Russia received $10,200,000 for a year from the same source. In April 1915 France received short-term credit of about $30,000,000 arranged by J. P. Morgan. Brown Bros. opened a commercial line of credit of $25,000,000 for French merchants in the summer of 1915.

In October 1915 America's bankers ceased distinguishing between credits and loans and the Government was helpless to prevent this. American investors began to finance the Allies in earnest with the flotation of the great Anglo-French loan of $500,000,000 through a huge banking syndicate headed by J. P. Morgan & Co. Similar loans followed fast, and by 1917 total loans and credits to the Allies of well over $2,000,000,000 were outstanding. Morgan & Co. had a demand loan or overdraft due from Great Britain of approximately $400,000,000, which obviously could not be paid at that time. Instead Great Britain desperately needed enormous new credits.

By this time the history of the bank credits up to October 1915 had been repeated – on a far larger scale. In the early part of 1917 it was clear that our private financial and banking resources were exhausted. Unless the great credit of the American Nation could itself be pledged, the flow of goods to Europe would end and the claims of our banks, who had made possible this flow of goods in the past, would not be paid. No one stopped to inquire whether new funds would not similarly be burned up in the holocaust of European war and would be used in the natural course of events to bail out the American banks. The facts are that by November 11, 1918, $7,000,000,000 were lent to Europe by our Government and, though most of this is still unpaid, the private loans were redeemed and the securities behind them have disappeared.

We are now discussing things that have heretofore been whispered only – things that most of us felt couldn't be true because they shouldn't be true. But if a recognition of ugly facts will help us prevent another disaster we must discuss them openly. . . .

The experience of the last war includes the lesson that neutral rights are not a matter for national protection unless we are prepared to protect them by force. Senator Clark and I, and, I believe, Representative Maverick and other colleagues in Congress, believe that the only hope of our staying out of war is through our people recognizing and declaring as a matter of considered and fervently held national policy, that we will not ship munitions to aid combatants and that those of our citizens who ship other materials to belligerent nations must do so at their own risk and without any hope of protection from our Government. If our financiers and industrialists wish to speculate for war profits, let them be warned in advance that they are to be limited to speculation with their own capital and not with the lives of their countrymen and the fabric of their whole nation.

We must, however, frankly face the cost which this kind of decision demands. We must be realists. It requires the giving up of part at least of our present trade balance. It will mean a loss of part of our present revenue from our merchant marine and from banking. More important still, it will mean the abandonment of really vast new profits held temptingly before us.

If we cannot give up these things we cannot hope for peace. I for one believe that great though this cost is, it is insignificant compared to the catastrophe of war. . . .

Congressional Record, 74th Congress, 2nd Session, Senate, May 28, 1935, pp. 8388–40

(b) *Text of the 'Neutrality Act' of August 31, 1935*

JOINT RESOLUTION

Providing for the prohibition of the export of arms, ammunition, and implements of war to belligerent countries; the prohibition of the transportation of arms, ammunition, and implements of war by vessels of the United States for the use of belligerent states; for the registration and licensing of persons engaged in the business of manufacturing, exporting, or importing arms, ammunition, or implements of war; and restricting travel by American citizens on belligerent ships during war.

Resolved by the Senate and House of Representatives of the United States of America in Congress assembled, That, upon the outbreak or during the progress of war between, or among, two or more foreign states, the President shall proclaim such fact, and it shall thereafter be unlawful to export arms, ammunition, or implements of war from any place in the United States, or possessions of the United States, to any port of such belligerent states, or to any neutral port for transshipment to, or for the use of, a belligerent country.

The President, by proclamation, shall definitely enumerate the arms, ammunition, or implements of war, the export of which is prohibited by this Act.

The President may, from time to time, by proclamation, extend such embargo upon the export of arms, ammunition, or implements of war to other states as and when they may become involved in such war.

Whoever, in violation of any of the provisions of this section, shall export, or attempt to export, or cause to be exported, arms, ammunition, or implements of war from the United States, or any of its possessions, shall be fined not more than $10,000 or imprisoned not more than five years, or both, and the property, vessel, or vehicle containing the same shall be subject to the provisions of sections 1 to 8, inclusive, title 6, chapter 30, of the Act approved June 15, 1917 (40 Stat. 223–225; U. S. C., title 22, secs. 238–245).

In the case of the forfeiture of any arms, ammunition, or implements of war by reason of a violation of this Act, no public or private sale shall be required; but such arms, ammunition, or implements of war shall be delivered to the Secretary of War for such use or disposal thereof as shall be approved by the President of the United States.

When in the judgment of the President the conditions which have caused him to issue his proclamation have ceased to exist he shall revoke the same and the provisions hereof shall thereupon cease to apply. . . .

SEC. 3. Whenever the President shall issue the proclamation provided for in section 1 of this Act, thereafter it shall be unlawful for any American vessel to carry any arms, ammunition, or implements of war to any port of the belligerent countries named in such proclamations as being at war, or to any neutral port for transshipment to, or for the use of, a belligerent country.

Whoever, in violation of the provisions of this section, shall take, attempt to take, or shall authorize, hire, or solicit another to take any such vessel carrying such cargo out of port or from the jurisdiction of the United States shall be fined not more than $10,000 or imprisoned not more than five years, or both; and, in addition, such vessel, her tackle, apparel, furniture, equipment, and the arms, ammunition, and implements of war on board shall be forfeited to the United States.

When the President finds the conditions which have caused him to issue his proclamation have ceased to exist, he shall revoke his proclamation, and the provisions of this section shall thereupon cease to apply....

SEC. 6. Whenever, during any war in which the United States is neutral, the President shall find that the maintenance of peace between the United States and foreign nations, or the protection of the lives of citizens of the United States, or the protection of the commercial interests of the United States and its citizens, or the security of the United States requires that the American citizens should refrain from traveling as passengers on the vessels of any belligerent nation, he shall so proclaim, and thereafter no citizen of the United States shall travel on any vessel of any belligerent nation except at his own risk, unless in accordance with such rules and regulations as the President shall prescribe: *Provided, however,* That the provisions of this section shall not apply to a citizen traveling on the vessel of a belligerent whose voyage was begun in advance of the date of the President's proclamation, and who had no opportunity to discontinue his voyage after that date: *And provided further,* That they shall not apply under ninety days after the date of the President's proclamation to a citizen returning from a foreign country to the United States or to any of its possessions. When, in the President's judgment, the conditions which have caused him to issue his proclamation have ceased to exist, he shall revoke his proclamation and the provisions of this section shall thereupon cease to apply....

Peace and War, pp. 266–71 (excerpts)

4 Address by President Roosevelt at Chautauqua, 1936

August 14, 1936

A few days ago I was asked what the subject of this talk would be, and I replied that ... I wanted to discuss the subject of peace ... because in the hurly-burly of domestic politics it is important that our people should not overlook problems and issues which, though they lie beyond our borders, may, and probably will, have a vital influence on the United States of the future.

Many who have visited me in Washington in the past few months may have been surprised when I have told them personally and because of my own daily contacts with all manner of difficult situations I am more concerned and less cheerful about international world conditions than about our immediate domestic prospects.

I say this to you not as a confirmed pessimist but as one who still hopes that envy, hatred, and malice among nations have reached their peak and will be succeeded by a new tide of peace and good will. I say this as one who has participated in many of the decisions of peace and war before, during, and after the World War; one who has traveled much, and one who has spent a goodly portion of every 24 hours in the study of foreign relations.

Long before I returned to Washington as President of the United States I had made up my mind that, pending what might be called a more opportune moment on other continents, the United States could best serve the cause of a peaceful humanity by setting an example. That was why on the 4th of March, 1933, I made the following declaration:

'In the field of world policy I would dedicate this nation to the policy of the good neighbor – the neighbor who resolutely respects himself and, because he does so, respects the rights of others – the neighbor who respects his obligations and respects the sanctity of his agreements in and with a world of neighbors.'

This declaration represents my purpose; but it represents more than a purpose, for it stands for a practice. To a measurable degree it has succeeded; the whole world now knows that the United States cherishes no predatory ambitions. We are strong; but less powerful nations know that they need not fear our strength. We seek no conquest: we stand for peace. ...

But, of necessity, we are deeply concerned about tendencies of recent years among many of the nations of other continents. It is a bitter experience to us when the spirit of agreements to which we are a party is not lived up to. It is an even more bitter experience for the whole company of nations to witness not only the spirit but the letter of international agreements violated with impunity and without regard to the simple principles of honor. Permanent friendships between nations as between men can be sustained only by scrupulous respect for the pledged word.

In spite of all this we have sought steadfastly to assist international movements to prevent war. We cooperated to the bitter end – and it was a bitter end – in the work of the General Disarmament Conference. When it failed we sought a separate treaty to deal with the manufacture of arms and the international traffic in arms. That proposal also came to nothing. We participated – again to the bitter end – in a conference to continue naval limitations, and, when it became evident that no general treaty could be signed because of the objections of other nations, we concluded with Great Britain and France a conditional treaty of qualitative limitations which, much to my regret, already shows signs of ineffectiveness.

We shun political commitments which might entangle us in foreign wars; we avoid connection with the political activities of the League of Nations; but I am glad to say that we have cooperated wholeheartedly in the social and humanitarian work at Geneva. Thus we are a part of the world effort to control traffic in narcotics, to improve international health, to help child welfare, to eliminate double taxation, and to better working conditions and laboring hours throughout the world.

We are not isolationists except insofar as we seek to isolate ourselves completely from war. Yet we must remember that so long as war exists on earth there will be some danger that even the nation which most ardently desires peace may be drawn into war.

I have seen war. I have seen war on land and sea. I have seen blood running from the wounded. I have seen men coughing out their gassed lungs. I have seen the dead in the mud. I have seen cities destroyed. I have seen 200 limping, exhausted men come out of line – the survivors of a regiment of 1,000 that went forward 48 hours before. I have seen children starving. I have seen the agony of mothers and wives. I hate war.

I have passed unnumbered hours, I shall pass unnumbered hours thinking and planning how war may be kept from this nation.

I wish I could keep war from all nations, but that is beyond my power. I can at least make certain that no act of the United States helps to produce or to promote war. I can at least make clear that the conscience of America revolts against war and that any nation which provokes war forfeits the sympathy of the people of the United States....

The Congress of the United States has given me certain authority to provide safeguards of American neutrality in case of war.

The President of the United States, who, under our Constitution, is vested with primary authority to conduct our international relations, thus has been given new weapons with which to maintain our neutrality.

Nevertheless – and I speak from a long experience – the effective maintenance of American neutrality depends today, as in the past, on the wisdom and determination of whoever at the moment occupy the offices of President and Secretary of State.

It is clear that our present policy and the measures passed by the Congress would, in the event of a war on some other continent, reduce war profits which would otherwise accrue to American citizens. Industrial and agricultural production for a war market may give immense fortunes to a few men; for the nation as a whole it produces disaster. It was the prospect of war profits that made our farmers in the west plow up prairie land that should never have been plowed but should have been left for grazing cattle. Today we are reaping the harvest of those war profits in the dust storms which have devastated those war-plowed areas.

It was the prospect of war profits that caused the extension of monopoly and unjustified expansion of industry and a price level so high that the normal relationship between debtor and creditor was destroyed.

Nevertheless, if war should break out again in another continent, let us not blink the fact that we would find in this country thousands of Americans who, seeking immediate riches – fools' gold – would attempt to break down or evade our neutrality.

They would tell you – and, unfortunately, their views would get wide publicity – that if they could produce and ship this and that and the other article to belligerent nations the unemployed of America would all find work. They would tell you that if they could extend credit to warring nations that credit would be used in the United States to build homes and factories and pay our debts. They would tell you that America once more would capture the trade of the world.

It would be hard to resist that clamor. It would be hard for many Americans, I fear, to look beyond, to realize the inevitable penalties, the inevitable day of reckoning that comes from a false prosperity. To resist the clamor of that greed, if war should come, would require the unswerving support of all Americans who love peace.

If we face the choice of profits or peace, the Nation will answer – must answer – 'we choose peace'. It is the duty of all of us to encourage such a body of public opinion in this country that the answer will be clear and for all practical purposes unanimous. . . .

We can keep out of war if those who watch and decide have a sufficiently detailed understanding of international affairs to make certain that the small decisions of each day do not lead toward war, and if, at the same time, they possess the courage to say 'no' to those who selfishly or unwisely would let us go to war.

Of all the nations of the world today we are in many ways most singularly blessed. Our closest neighbors are good neighbors. If there are remoter nations that wish us not good but ill, they know that we are strong; they know that we can and will defend ourselves and defend our neighborhood.

We seek to dominate no other nation. We ask no territorial expansion. We oppose imperialism. We desire reduction in world armaments.

We believe in democracy; we believe in freedom; we believe in peace. We offer to every nation of the world the handclasp of the good neighbor. Let those who wish our friendship look us in the eye and take our hand.

Peace and War, pp. 323–9 (excerpts)

5 The Basic Principles of American Foreign Policy

Address by Secretary of State Cordell Hull, Washington, March 17, 1938

The primary objectives of our foreign policy are the maintenance of the peace of our country and the promotion of the economic, the social, and the moral welfare of our people. Unfortunately, the means of attaining these objectives involve today so many factors of great complexity that their real significance is frequently misunderstood and misinterpreted.

By instinct and tradition our country has been, throughout its history, sincerely devoted to the cause of peace. Within the limitations imposed by time and circumstance we have earnestly sought to discharge our responsibilities as a member of the family of nations in promoting conditions essential to the maintenance of peace. We have consistently believed in the sanctity of treaty obligations and have endeavored to apply this belief in the actual practice of our foreign relations. In common with all other nations we have, since the end of the World War, assumed a solemn obligation not to resort to force as an instrument of national policy. All this gives us a moral right to express our deep concern over the rising tide of lawlessness, the growing disregard of treaties, the increasing reversion to the use of force, and the numerous other ominous tendencies which are emerging in the sphere of international relations.

On July 16, 1937, I issued a public statement setting forth the fundamental principles to which our Government adheres in the formulation of its foreign policy. On behalf of our Government I transmitted a copy of this statement to every government of the world, requesting such comment as each might see fit to offer. To our profound gratification an overwhelming majority of those governments joined in affirming their faith in these vital principles.

The most important of these principles, which are indispensable to a satisfactory international order, are as follows:

Maintenance of peace should be constantly advocated and practiced.

All nations should, through voluntary self-restraint, abstain from use of force in pursuit of policy and from interference in the internal affairs of other nations.

All nations should seek to adjust problems arising in their international relations by processes of peaceful negotiation and agreement.

All nations should uphold the principle of the sanctity of treaties and of faithful observance of international agreements.

Modification of provisions of treaties, when need therefor arises, should be by orderly processes carried out in a spirit of mutual helpfulness and accommodation.

Each nation should respect the rights of others and perform scrupulously its own established obligations; in brief, international law and the spirit which underlies it must be revitalized and strengthened.

Steps should be taken toward promotion of economic security and stability the world over through lowering or removal of barriers to international trade, according of effective equality of commercial opportunity, and application of the principle of equality of commercial treatment.

National armaments should be limited and be progressively reduced; at the same time, realizing the necessity for maintaining armed forces adequate for national security, each nation should to that end be prepared to reduce or increase its own armed forces in proportion as reductions or increases are made by other nations.

Apart from the question of alliances with others, each nation should be prepared to engage in cooperative effort, by peaceful and practicable means, in support of these principles.

The peace and progress of every nation are just as dependent on international law and order, based upon the foregoing principles, as the welfare, stability, and progress of a community are dependent upon domestic law and order, based upon legal, moral, and other recognized standards of conduct. No government faithful to the sacred trust involved in the task of providing for the safety and well-being of its people can disregard these universal principles. Every nation, whatever its form of government, can support them. Every nation must support them, if civilization is to survive. The longer the nations delay acceptance and observance of these fundamental tenets of constructive statesmanship, the graver will be the jeopardy into which all worth-while international relationships will be plunged, and with them the welfare, the happiness, and the civilized existence of all nations.

The crucial issue today is whether these principles will be vitalized and be firmly established as the foundation of an international order or whether international anarchy based on brute force will inundate the world and ultimately sweep away the very bases of civilization and progress. That issue is universal. No more than a community or a nation, can the world base its existence in part on law and in part on lawlessness, in part on order and in part on chaos, in part on processes of peace and in part on methods of violence. . . .

In announcing our intention to afford appropriate and reasonable protection to our rights and interests in the Far East, I stated clearly that we are fully determined to avoid the extremes either of internationalism or of isolationism. Internationalism would mean undesirable political involvements; isolationism would either compel us to confine all activities of our people within our own frontiers, with incalculable injury to the standard of living and the general welfare of our people, or else expose our nationals and our legitimate interests abroad to injustice or outrage wherever lawless conditions arise. Steering a sound middle course between these two extremes, we are convinced that a policy of affording appropriate protection – under the rule of reason, in such form as may be best suited to the particular circumstances, and in accordance with the principles we advocate – is imperatively needed to serve our national interest.

Our decision in this matter is based not only on what we firmly believe to be a specific and elementary duty of a government toward its citizens, but also on other and broader considerations. Respect by a country for the rights and interests of others is a visible test of the fulfillment of obligations assumed by virtue of acceptance of international law and of undertakings embodied in negotiated international instruments. It is, therefore, a test of the observance of those fundamental principles of civilized relations among nations, which, if firmly established, provide in themselves the best means of protection against violation and abuse of the legitimate rights and interests of every nation.

To waive rights and to permit interests to lapse in the face of their actual or threatened violation – and thereby to abandon obligations – in any important area of the world, can serve only to encourage disregard of law and of the basic principles of international order, and thus contribute to the inevitable spread of international anarchy throughout the world. For this country, as for any country, to act in such manner *anywhere* would be to invite disregard and violation of its rights and interests *everywhere*, by every nation so inclined, large or small. . . .

We have affirmed on every possible occasion and have urged upon all nations the supreme need for keeping alive and for practicing sound fundamental principles of relations among civilized nations. We have never entertained and we have not the slightest intention to entertain any such notion as the use of American armed forces for 'policing the world'. But we equally have not the slightest intention of reversing a tradition of a century and a half by abandoning our deep concern for, and our advocacy of, the establishment everywhere of international order under law, based upon the well-recognized principles to which I have referred. It is our profound conviction that the most effective contribution which we, as a nation sincerely devoted to the cause of peace, can make – in the tragic conditions with which our people, in common with the rest of mankind, are confronted today – is to have this country respected throughout the world for integrity, justice, good will, strength, and unswerving loyalty to principles.

The foregoing is the essence of our foreign policy. The record is an open book. We spare no effort to make known the facts regarding our attitude, our objectives, and our acts. . . .

We want to live in a world which is at peace; in which the forces of militarism, of territorial aggression, and of international anarchy in general will become utterly odious, revolting, and intolerable to the conscience of mankind; in which the doctrine of order under law will be firmly established; in which there will no longer be one code of morality, honor, justice, and fair play for the individual in his relations with other individuals, and an entirely different code for governments and nations in their relations with each other. We want to live in a world in which fruitful and constructive international relationships can serve as a medium for disseminating throughout the world the benefits of the material, spiritual, and moral progress of mankind.

To that end we will continue to give full and sincere adherence to the fundamental principles which underlie international order; we will continue to urge universal acceptance and observance of these principles; we will continue, wherever necessary and in every practicable and peaceful way, to cooperate with other nations which are actuated by the same desires and are pursuing the same objectives; we will persevere in appropriate efforts to safeguard our legitimate rights and interests in every part of the world; and we will, while scrupulously respecting the rights of others, insist on their respecting our rights. . . .

Peace and War, pp. 407-19 (excerpts)

6 The United States and the Munich Crisis

Telegram from President Roosevelt to Adolf Hitler, September 27, 1938

I desire to acknowledge Your Excellency's reply to my telegram of September 26. I was confident that you would coincide in the opinion I expressed regarding the unforeseeable consequences and the incalculable disaster which would result to the entire world from the outbreak of a European war.

The question before the world today, Mr. Chancellor, is not the question of errors of judgment or of injustices committed in the past. It is the question of the fate of the world today and tomorrow. The world asks of us who at this moment are heads of nations the supreme capacity to achieve the destinies of nations without forcing upon them as a price, the mutilation and death of millions of citizens.

Resort to force in the Great War failed to bring tranquillity. Victory and defeat were alike sterile. That lesson the world should have learned. For that reason above all others I addressed on September 26 my appeal to Your Excellency and to the President of Czechoslovakia and to the Prime Ministers of Great Britain and of France.

The two points I sought to emphasize were, first, that all matters of difference between the German Government and the Czechoslovak Government could and should be settled by pacific methods; and, second, that the threatened alternative of the use of force on a scale likely to result in a general war is as unnecessary as it is unjustifiable. It is, therefore, supremely important that negotiations should continue without interruption until a fair and constructive solution is reached.

My conviction on these two points is deepened because responsible statesmen have officially stated that an agreement in principle has already been reached between the Government of the German Reich and the Government of Czechoslovakia, although the precise time, method and detail of carrying out that agreement remain at issue.

Whatever existing differences may be, and whatever their merits may be – and upon them I do not and need not undertake to pass – my appeal was solely that negotiations be continued until a peaceful settlement is found, and that thereby a resort to force be avoided.

Present negotiations still stand open. They can be continued if you will give the word. Should the need for supplementing them become evident, nothing stands in the way of widening their scope into a conference of all the nations directly interested in the present controversy. Such a meeting to be held immediately – in some neutral spot in Europe – would offer the opportunity for this and correlated questions to be solved in a spirit of justice, of fair dealing, and, in all human probability, with greater permanence.

In my considered judgment, and in the light of the experience of this century, continued negotiations remain the only way by which the immediate problem can be disposed of upon any lasting basis.

Should you agree to a solution in this peaceful manner I am convinced that hundreds of millions throughout the world would recognize your action as an outstanding historic service to all humanity.

Allow me to state my unqualified conviction that history, and the souls of every man, woman, and child whose lives will be lost in the threatened war will hold us and all of us accountable should we omit any appeal for its prevention.

The Government of the United States has no political involvements in Europe, and will assume no obligations in the conduct of the present negotiations. Yet in our own right we recognize our responsibilities as a part of a world of neighbors.

The conscience and the impelling desire of the people of my country demand that the voice of their government be raised again and yet again to avert and to avoid war.

Peace and War, pp. 428-9 (excerpts)

7 'The Great Commitment'

Address by President Roosevelt at the University of Virginia, June 10, 1940

... Perception of danger, danger to our institutions, may come slowly or it may come with a rush and a shock as it has to the people of the

United States in the past few months. This perception of danger, danger in a world-wide area – it has come to us clearly and overwhelmingly – we perceive the peril in a world-wide arena, an arena that may become so narrowed that only the Americas will retain the ancient faiths.

Some indeed still hold to the now somewhat obvious delusion that we of the United States can safely permit the United States to become a lone island, a lone island in a world dominated by the philosophy of force.

Such an island may be the dream of those who still talk and vote as isolationists. Such an island represents to me and to the overwhelming majority of Americans today a helpless nightmare, the helpless nightmare of a people without freedom; yes, the nightmare of a people lodged in prison, handcuffed, hungry, and fed through the bars from day to day by the contemptuous, unpitying masters of other continents.

It is natural also that we should ask ourselves how now we can prevent the building of that prison and the placing of ourselves in the midst of it.

Let us not hesitate – all of us – to proclaim certain truths. Overwhelmingly we, as a Nation – and this applies to all the other American nations – are convinced that military and naval victory for the gods of force and hate would endanger the institutions of democracy in the western world, and that equally, therefore, the whole of our sympathies lies with those nations that are giving their life blood in combat against these forces.

The people and the Government of the United States have seen with the utmost regret and with grave disquiet the decision of the Italian Government to engage in the hostilities now raging in Europe.

More than 3 months ago the Chief of the Italian Government sent me word that because of the determination of Italy to limit, so far as might be possible, the spread of the European conflict, more than 200 millions of people in the region of the Mediterranean had been enabled to escape the suffering and the devastation of war.

I informed the Chief of the Italian Government that this desire on the part of Italy to prevent the war from spreading met with full sympathy and response on the part of the Government and the people of the United States, and I expressed the earnest hope of this Government and of this people that this policy on the part of Italy might be continued. I made it clear that in the opinion of the Government of the United States any extension of hostilities in the region of the Mediterranean might result in a still greater enlargement of the scene of the conflict, the conflict in the Near East and in Africa, and that if this came to pass no one could foretell how much greater the theater of the war eventually might become. . . .

This Government directed its efforts to doing what it could to work for the preservation of peace in the Mediterranean area, and it likewise expressed its willingness to endeavor to cooperate with the Government of Italy when the appropriate occasion arose for the creation of a more stable world order, through the reduction of armaments and through the construction of a more liberal international economic system which would assure to all powers equality of opportunity in the world's markets and in the securing of raw materials on equal terms.

I have likewise, of course, felt it necessary in my communications to Signor Mussolini to express the concern of the Government of the United States because of the fact that any extension of the war in the region of the Mediterranean would inevitably result in great prejudice to the ways of life and government and to the trade and commerce of all of the American republics.

The Government of Italy has now chosen to preserve what it terms its 'freedom of action' and to fulfill what it states are its promises to Germany. In so doing it has manifested disregard for the rights and security of other nations, disregard for the lives of the peoples of those nations which are directly threatened by this spread of the war; and has evidenced its unwillingness to find the means through pacific negotiations for the satisfaction of what it believes are its legitimate aspirations.

On this tenth day of June 1940, the hand that held the dagger has struck it into the back of its neighbor.

On this tenth day of June 1940, in this University founded by the first great American teacher of democracy, we send forth our prayers and our hopes to those beyond the seas who are maintaining with magnificent valor their battle for freedom.

In our, in our unity, in our American unity, we will pursue two obvious and simultaneous courses; we will extend to the opponents of force the material resources of this Nation and, at the same time, we will harness and speed up the use of those resources in order that we ourselves in the Americas may have equipment and training equal to the task of any emergency and every defense.

All roads leading to the accomplishment of these objectives must be kept clear of obstructions. We will not slow down or detour. Signs and signals call for speed – full speed ahead.

Yes, it is right that each new generation should ask questions. But in recent months the principal question has been somewhat simplified. Once more the future of the Nation, the future of the American people is at stake.

We need not and we will not, in any way, abandon our continuing effort to make democracy work within our borders. Yes, we still insist on the need for vast improvements in our own social and economic life.

But that, that is a component part of national defense itself.

The program unfolds swiftly, and into that program will fit the responsibility and the opportunity of every man and woman in the land to preserve his and her heritage in days of peril.

I call for effort, courage, sacrifice, devotion. Granting the love of freedom, all of these are possible.

And – and the love of freedom is still fierce, still steady in the Nation today.

Peace and War, pp. 545–9 (excerpts)

8 American Aid to Britain : the Destroyers-Bases Exchange

Message from President Roosevelt to the Congress, September 3, 1940

I transmit herewith for the information of the Congress notes exchanged between the British Ambassador at Washington and the Secretary of State on September 2, 1940, under which this Government has acquired the right to lease naval and air bases in Newfoundland, and in the islands of Bermuda, the Bahamas, Jamaica, St. Lucia, Trinidad, and Antigua, and in British Guiana; also a copy of an opinion of the Attorney General dated August 27, 1940, regarding my authority to consummate this arrangement.

The right to bases in Newfoundland and Bermuda are gifts – generously given and gladly received. The other bases mentioned have been acquired in exchange for fifty of our over-age destroyers.

This is not inconsistent in any sense with our status of peace. Still less is it a threat against any nation. It is an epochal and far-reaching act of preparation for continental defense in the face of grave danger.

Preparation for defense is an inalienable prerogative of a sovereign state. Under present circumstances this exercise of sovereign right is essential to the maintenance of our peace and safety. This is the most important action in the reinforcement of our national defense that has been taken since the Louisiana Purchase. Then as now, considerations of safety from overseas attack were fundamental.

The value to the Western Hemisphere of these outposts of security is beyond calculation. Their need has long been recognized by our country, and especially by those primarily charged with the duty of charting and organizing our own naval and military defense. They are essential to the protection of the Panama Canal, Central America, the Northern portion of South America, The Antilles, Canada, Mexico, and our own Eastern and Gulf Seaboards. Their consequent importance in hemispheric defense is obvious. For these reasons I have taken advantage of the present opportunity to acquire them.

Peace and War, pp. 564-5

9 Lend-Lease

Address by President Roosevelt to the Congress, January 6, 1941

I address you, the Members of the Seventy-seventh Congress, at a moment unprecedented in the history of the Union. I use the word 'unprecedented', because at no previous time has American security been as seriously threatened from without as it is today.

Our national policy is this:

First, by an impressive expression of the public will and without regard to partisanship, we are committed to all-inclusive national defense.

Second, by an impressive expression of the public will and without regard to partisanship, we are committed to full support of all those resolute peoples, everywhere, who are resisting aggression and are thereby keeping war away from our hemisphere. By this support, we express our determination that the democratic cause shall prevail; and we strengthen the defense and security of our own Nation.

Third, by an impressive expression of the public will and without regard to partisanship, we are committed to the proposition that principles of morality and considerations for our own security will never permit us to acquiesce in a peace dictated by aggressors and sponsored by appeasers. We know that enduring peace cannot be bought at the cost of other people's freedom.

In the recent national election there was no substantial difference between the two great parties in respect to that national policy. No issue was fought out on this line before the American electorate. Today, it is abundantly evident that American citizens everywhere are demanding and supporting speedy and complete action in recognition of obvious danger.

Therefore, the immediate need is a swift and driving increase in our armament production.

To change a whole nation from a basis of peacetime production of implements of peace to a basis of wartime production of implements of war is no small task. And the greatest difficulty comes at the beginning of the program, when new tools and plant facilities and new assembly lines and shipways must first be constructed before the actual matériel begins to flow steadily and speedily from them.

The Congress, of course, must rightly keep itself informed at all times of the progress of the program. However, there is certain information, as the Congress itself will readily recognize, which, in the interests of our own security and those of the nations we are supporting, must of needs be kept in confidence.

New circumstances are constantly begetting new needs for our safety. I shall ask this Congress for greatly increased new appropriations and authorizations to carry on what we have begun.

I also ask this Congress for authority and for funds sufficient to manufacture additional munitions and war supplies of many kinds, to be turned over to those nations which are now in actual war with aggressor nations.

Our most useful and immediate role is to act as an arsenal for them as well as for ourselves. They do not need man power. They do need billions of dollars worth of the weapons of defense.

The time is near when they will not be able to pay for them in ready cash. We cannot, and will not, tell them they must surrender, merely because of present inability to pay for the weapons which we know they must have.

I do not recommend that we make them a loan of dollars with which to pay for these weapons – a loan to be repaid in dollars.

I recommend that we make it possible for those nations to continue to obtain war materials in the United States, fitting their orders into our own program. Nearly all of their matériel would, if the time ever came, be useful for our own defense.

Taking counsel of expert military and naval authorities, considering what is best for our own security, we are free to decide how much should be kept here and how much should be sent abroad to our friends who by their determined and heroic resistance are giving us time in which to make ready our own defense.

For what we send abroad, we shall be repaid, within a reasonable time following the close of hostilities, in similar materials, or, at our option, in other goods of many kinds which they can produce and which we need.

Let us say to the democracies: 'We Americans are vitally concerned in your defense of freedom. We are putting forth our energies, our resources, and our organizing powers to give you the strength to regain and maintain a free world. We shall send you, in ever-increasing numbers, ships, planes, tanks, guns. This is our purpose and our pledge.'

In fulfillment of this purpose we will not be intimidated by the threats of dictators that they will regard as a breach of international law and as an act of war our aid to the democracies which dare to resist their aggression. Such aid is not an act of war, even if a dictator should unilaterally proclaim it so to be.

When the dictators are ready to make war upon us, they will not wait for an act of war on our part. They did not wait for Norway or Belgium or the Netherlands to commit an act of war.

Their only interest is in a new one-way international law, which lacks mutuality in its observance, and, therefore, becomes an instrument of oppression.

The happiness of future generations of Americans may well depend upon how effective and how immediate we can make our aid felt. No one can tell the exact character of the emergency situations that we may be called upon to meet. The Nation's hands must not be tied when the Nation's life is in danger.

We must all prepare to make the sacrifices that the emergency – as serious as war itself – demands. Whatever stands in the way of speed and efficiency in defense preparations must give way to the national need.

A free nation has the right to expect full cooperation from all groups. A free nation has the right to look to the leaders of business, of labor, and of agriculture to take the lead in stimulating effort, not among other groups but within their own groups.

I have called for personal sacrifice. I am assured of the willingness of almost all Americans to respond to that call.

A part of the sacrifice means the payment of more money in taxes. In my Budget message I recommend that a greater portion of this great defense program be paid for from taxation than we are paying today. No person should try, or be allowed, to get rich out of this program; and the principle of tax payments in accordance with ability to pay should be constantly before our eyes to guide our legislation.

If the Congress maintains these principles, the voters, putting patriotism ahead of pocketbooks, will give you their applause.

In the future days, which we seek to make secure, we look forward to a world founded upon four essential human freedoms.

The first is freedom of speech and expression – everywhere in the world.

The second is freedom of every person to worship God in his own way – everywhere in the world.

The third is freedom from want – which, translated into world terms, means economic understandings which will secure to every nation a healthy peacetime life for its inhabitants – everywhere in the world.

The fourth is freedom from fear – which, translated into world terms, means a world-wide reduction of armaments to such a point and in such a thorough fashion that no nation will be in a position to commit an act of physical aggression against any neighbor – anywhere in the world.

That is no vision of a distant millennium. It is a definite basis for a kind of world attainable in our own time and generation. That kind of world is the very antithesis of the so-called new order of tyranny which the dictators seek to create with the crash of a bomb.

To that new order we oppose the greater conception – the moral order. A good society is able to face schemes of world domination and foreign revolutions alike without fear.

Since the beginning of our American history we have been engaged in change – in a perpetual peaceful revolution – a revolution which goes on steadily, quietly adjusting itself to changing conditions – without the concentration camp or the quick-lime in the ditch. The world order which we seek is the cooperation of free countries, working together in a friendly, civilized society.

This Nation has placed its destiny in the hands and heads and hearts of its millions of free men and women; and its faith in freedom under the guidance of God. Freedom means the supremacy of human rights everywhere. Our support goes to those who struggle to gain those rights or keep them. Our strength is in our unity of purpose.

To that high concept there can be no end save victory.

Peace and War, pp. 608–11

10 Towards a Shooting War in the Atlantic

Radio Address of President Roosevelt, September 11, 1941

The Navy Department of the United States has reported to me that on the morning of September fourth the United States destroyer *Greer*, proceeding in full daylight towards Iceland, had reached a point south-east of Greenland. She was carrying American mail to Iceland. She was flying the American flag. Her identity as an American ship was unmistakable.

She was then and there attacked by a submarine. Germany admits that it was a German submarine. The submarine deliberately fired a torpedo at the *Greer*, followed later by another torpedo attack. In spite of what Hitler's propaganda bureau has invented, and in spite of what any American obstructionist organization may prefer to believe, I tell you the blunt fact that the German submarine fired first upon this American destroyer without warning, and with deliberate design to sink her.

Our destroyer, at the time, was in waters which the Government of the United States had declared to be waters of self-defense – surrounding outposts of American protection in the Atlantic.

In the north, outposts have been established by us in Iceland, Greenland, Labrador, and Newfoundland. Through these waters there pass many ships of many flags. They bear food and other supplies to civilians; and they bear matériel of war, for which the people of the United States are spending billions of dollars, and which, by congressional action, they have declared to be essential for the defense of their own land.

The United States destroyer, when attacked, was proceeding on a legitimate mission.

If the destroyer was visible to the submarine when the torpedo was fired, then the attack was a deliberate attempt by the Nazis to sink a clearly identified American warship. On the other hand, if the submarine was beneath the surface and, with the aid of its listening devices, fired in the direction of the sound of the American destroyer without even taking the trouble to learn its identity – as the official German communiqué would indicate – then the attack was even more outrageous. For it indicates a policy of indiscriminate violence against any vessel sailing the seas – belligerent or non-belligerent.

This was piracy – legally and morally. It was not the first nor the last act of piracy which the Nazi Government has committed against the American flag in this war. Attack has followed attack.

A few months ago an American-flag merchant ship, the *Robin Moor*, was sunk by a Nazi submarine in the middle of the South Atlantic, under circumstances violating long-established international law and every principle of humanity. The passengers and the crew were forced into open boats hundreds of miles from land, in direct violation of international agreements signed by the Government of Germany. No apology, no allegation of mistake, no offer of reparations has come from the Nazi Government. . . .

In the face of all this, we Americans are keeping our feet on the ground. Our type of democratic civilization has outgrown the thought of feeling compelled to fight some other nation by reason of any single piratical attack on one of our ships. We are not becoming hysterical or losing our sense of proportion. Therefore, what I am thinking and saying does not relate to any isolated episode.

Instead, we Americans are taking a long-range point of view in regard to certain fundamentals and to a series of events on land and on sea which must be considered as a whole – as a part of a world pattern.

It would be unworthy of a great nation to exaggerate an isolated incident or to become inflamed by some one act of violence. But it would be inexcusable folly to minimize such incidents in the face of evidence which makes it clear that the incident is not isolated but part of a general plan.

The important truth is that these acts of international lawlessness are a manifestation of a design which has been made clear to the American people for a long time. It is the Nazi design to abolish the freedom of the seas and to acquire absolute control and domination of the seas for themselves.

For with control of the seas in their own hands, the way can become clear for their next step – domination of the United States and the Western Hemisphere by force. Under Nazi control of the seas, no merchant ship of the United States or of any other American republic would be free to carry on any peaceful commerce, except by the condescending grace of this foreign and tyrannical power. The Atlantic Ocean which has been, and which should always be, a free and friendly highway for us would then become a deadly menace to the commerce of the United States, to the coasts of the United States, and to the inland cities of the United States.

The Hitler Government, in defiance of the laws of the sea and of the recognized rights of all other nations, has presumed to declare, on paper, that great areas of the seas – even including a vast expanse lying in the Western Hemisphere – are to be closed, and that no ships may enter them for any purpose, except at peril of being sunk. Actually they are sinking ships at will and without warning in widely separated areas both within and far outside of these far-flung pretended zones.

This Nazi attempt to seize control of the oceans is but a counterpart of the Nazi plots now being carried on throughout the Western

Hemisphere – all designed toward the same end. For Hitler's advance guards – not only his avowed agents but also his dupes among us – have sought to make ready for him footholds and bridgeheads in the New World, to be used as soon as he has gained control of the oceans.

His intrigues, his plots, his machinations, his sabotage in this New World are all known to the Government of the United States. Conspiracy has followed conspiracy.

Last year a plot to seize the Government of Uruguay was smashed by the prompt action of that country, which was supported in full by her American neighbors. A like plot was then hatching in Argentina, and that Government has carefully and wisely blocked it at every point. More recently, an endeavor was made to subvert the Government of Bolivia. Within the past few weeks the discovery was made of secret air-landing fields in Colombia, within easy range of the Panama Canal. I could multiply instances. . . .

Generation after generation, America has battled for the general policy of the freedom of the seas. That policy is a very simple one – but a basic, fundamental one. It means that no nation has the right to make the broad oceans of the world, at great distance from the actual theater of land war, unsafe for the commerce of others.

That has been our policy, proved time and time again, in all our history.

Our policy has applied from time immemorial – and still applies – not merely to the Atlantic but to the Pacific and to all other oceans as well.

Unrestricted submarine warfare in 1941 constitutes a defiance – an act of aggression – against that historic American policy.

It is now clear that Hitler has begun his campaign to control the seas by ruthless force and by wiping out every vestige of international law and humanity. . . .

This attack on the *Greer* was no localized military operation in the North Atlantic. This was no mere episode in a struggle between two nations. This was one determined step towards creating a permanent world system based on force, terror, and murder.

And I am sure that even now the Nazis are waiting to see whether the United States will by silence give them the green light to go ahead on this path of destruction.

The Nazi danger to our Western World has long ceased to be a mere possibility. The danger is here now – not only from a military enemy but from an enemy of all law, all liberty, all morality, all religion.

There has now come a time when you and I must see the cold,

inexorable necessity of saying to these inhuman, unrestrained seekers of world-conquest and permanent world-domination by the sword – 'You seek to throw our children and our children's children into your form of terrorism and slavery. You have now attacked our own safety. You shall go no further.'

Normal practices of diplomacy – note-writing – are of no possible use in dealing with international outlaws who sink our ships and kill our citizens.

One peaceful nation after another has met disaster because each refused to look the Nazi danger squarely in the eye until it actually had them by the throat.

The United States will not make that fatal mistake.

No act of violence or intimidation will keep us from maintaining intact two bulwarks of defense: first, our line of supply of matériel to the enemies of Hitler; and second, the freedom of our shipping on the high seas.

No matter what it takes, no matter what it costs, we will keep open the line of legitimate commerce in these defensive waters.

We have sought no shooting war with Hitler. We do not seek it now. But neither do we want peace so much that we are willing to pay for it by permitting him to attack our naval and merchant ships while they are on legitimate business.

I assume that the German leaders are not deeply concerned by what we Americans say or publish about them. We cannot bring about the downfall of Nazism by the use of long-range invective.

But when you see a rattlesnake poised to strike, you do not wait until he has struck before you crush him.

These Nazi submarines and raiders are the rattlesnakes of the Atlantic. They are a menace to the free pathways of the high seas. They are a challenge to our sovereignty. They hammer at our most precious rights when they attack ships of the American flag – symbols of our independence, our freedom, our very life.

It is clear to all Americans that the time has come when the Americas themselves must now be defended. A continuation of attacks in our own waters, or in waters which could be used for further and greater attacks on us, will inevitably weaken American ability to repel Hitlerism.

Do not let us split hairs. Let us not ask ourselves whether the Americas should begin to defend themselves after the fifth attack, or the tenth attack, or the twentieth attack.

The time for active defense is now.

Do not let us split hairs. Let us not say – 'We will only defend ourselves if the torpedo succeeds in getting home, or if the crew and the passengers are drowned.'

This is the time for prevention of attack.

If submarines or raiders attack in distant waters, they can attack equally well within sight of our own shores. Their very presence in any waters which America deems vital to its defense constitutes an attack.

In the waters which we deem necessary for our defense, American naval vessels and American planes will no longer wait until Axis submarines lurking under the water, or Axis raiders on the surface of the sea, strike their deadly blow – first.

Upon our naval and air patrol – now operating in large number over a vast expanse of the Atlantic Ocean – falls the duty of maintaining the American policy of freedom of the seas – now. That means, very simply and clearly, that our patrolling vessels and planes will protect all merchant ships – not only American ships but ships of any flag – engaged in commerce in our defensive waters. . . .

My obligation as President is historic; it is clear; it is inescapable.

It is no act of war on our part when we decide to protect the seas which are vital to American defense. The aggression is not ours. Ours is solely defense.

But let this warning be clear. From now on, if German or Italian vessels of war enter the waters the protection of which is necessary for American defense they do so at their own peril.

The orders which I have given as Commander-in-Chief to the United States Army and Navy are to carry out that policy – at once.

The sole responsibility rests upon Germany. There will be no shooting unless Germany continues to seek it.

That is my obvious duty in this crisis. That is the clear right of this sovereign nation. That is the only step possible, if we would keep tight the wall of defense which we are pledged to maintain around this Western Hemisphere.

I have no illusions about the gravity of this step. I have not taken it hurriedly or lightly. It is the result of months and months of constant thought and anxiety and prayer. In the protection of your Nation and mine it cannot be avoided. . . .

Peace and War, pp. 737–43 (excerpts)

11 The Isolationist Attack

(a) *Former President Herbert Hoover: 'We Must Keep Out', article in* Saturday Evening Post, *October 27, 1939*

The American people will be confronted with the issue of war or peace as long as this war in Europe lasts. That is the most fateful issue that can come to a people. Each generation faces new issues, new problems, and seeks new solutions. But the invisible forces which make war, peace, and revolution are old, and they repeat. And to make sound progress nations, like individuals, must test their solutions with the stern and often inhibiting measure of human experience. And like individuals, the memories of nations are sometimes short.

I spent nearly a score of years from the outbreak of the Great War in 1914, dealing with these forces, and I may sum my conclusions at once: America must keep out of these wars. It can keep out of these wars. It has nothing to fear for our own independence from the result of these wars. This is no case of 'hope' that we may stay out of war; it is the time for will and inflexible resolution to stay out. Our greatest service is a strong America to aid the rebuilding of a European world which will be tottering no matter who the victors in this war may be. Our greatest service to civilization is to put our own house in order and maintain true liberty upon this continent. For it may be that otherwise liberty will sink for centuries in the night of despair.

War and peace are not cold mathematical problems. Our decisions will be determined by our emotions as well as our reason. Today we have two dominant attitudes. We are against joining in the European and Asiatic wars. That attitude is the dominance of reason. We are incensed at the dictatorships, their ideologies, and their aggressions. We sympathize with Great Britain, France, and Poland. Our danger is that our indignation will displace our reason.

WHAT MAKES WAR IN EUROPE

First, let us examine the invisible forces which drive the fates in Europe.

To many American eyes Europe consists of magnificent cities, historic cathedrals, art, music, literature, great universities, monuments of human heroism and progress. It possesses peoples of fine hospitality, of the widest cultivation and attainments. For four centuries since the Renaissance men in Europe have fought and died to build the structure of personal liberty, to lift the dignity of men, to bring security and peace. And from every country – England, Germany, France, Russia, and all the others – we have received magnificent inheritances of human thought upon which our civilization has built.

But Americans too often see little of the gigantic but invisible forces of disintegration that so often dominate these peoples. Here are 26 races of 400,000,000 people, outside of Russia, living cheek by jowl in an area two-thirds the size of the United States. Through them surge the forces of nationalism, of imperialism, of age-old hates, memories of deep wrongs, fierce distrusts, and impellent fears. There are the conflicts of religions and persecution. Long before the World War these forces were in added ferment because of new ideas from the industrial revolution. There is here a hell's brew of malign spirits.

And these spirits find tangible expression in the rivalry of economic development, the setting up of barriers of trade, the struggles for political independence, the pressures of population, the grabs and quarrels over vast areas of the earth for colonization and for exploitation. These all add to the centrifugal forces.

The existence of great areas of mixed populations makes exact boundaries between nations almost hopeless. In every one of these zones some races are separated from their fatherland. On both sides the existing governments unceasingly seek to impose their national language and customs upon these minorities. The outcries of these oppressed to the sympathies of their racial brothers across the borders are unceasing stimulants to friction. And these boundaries shift from every war and the conflicts flame up in new areas.

To all this must be added the destruction of the last war and the loosening of moral restraints.

And periodically there boils up among these peoples some Pied Piper with silver tongue calling some new Utopia, or some man on horseback calls followers to wars of aggression. History, even since the foundation of our Republic, has been a succession of Napoleons, Kaiser Wilhelms, Lenins, Stalins, and Hitlers.

Resistant against all these furies are the benign forces of human liberty, of religion, of education, and of morals which have fought these evils over centuries. And among these peoples are great leaders of thought and of men, whose aspirations and whose life services have been given to allay these evils and to build up hope and faith and peace.

Yet, with a vicious rhythm, these malign forces seem to concentrate at some spot and drive peoples, like the Gadarene swine, over the precipice of war.

During the whole of our relations with them, Europe has had only intervals of unstable peace. It has lived always on a war footing. Its periods of peace have been a groping for a balance of power through groups and alliances based upon fear and upon arms.

The job of European statesmen of good will is to engage incessantly in power politics, by which aggression is checked and the malign forces allayed, in order that tenuous peace can be extended a little longer. It is a delicate job in which loyalties to agreement by any of them constantly give way to expediences and self-preservation.

As the years have gone on, with the growth of economic interdependence, of communications between nations, of power in weapons, all the world has been affected more and more by these wars in Europe and their destructions. The interest and sympathies of nations 5000 miles away are enlisted. Our own people suffer in unemployment and misery from this world dislocation. The effect of European wars upon early American life was but a faint echo of the thunderous blows we receive today.

We, therefore, are increasingly sensitive to every force that moves Europe, for good or evil. And we have our opinions about these forces. But being 3000 miles away, unable to appraise their movements in half a billion people, with our own form of government based upon slow-moving public opinion, idealistic in its approach and impossible of continuity in foreign policy, with racially divided emotions, we are wholly unequipped to take part in the hourly shifting power politics.

The voice of experience calls out sternly that we cannot solve the problems of, or keep the peace in, Europe. . . .

A WORLD WHERE NATIONAL INTEREST COMES FIRST

What have been the attitudes of Europe toward us during this period since the Great War?

Has Europe ever indicated that she would be willing to sacrifice one single small item that might be helpful to us?

After the armistice, when we need not have parted with a dollar, our government loaned huge amounts of our taxpayers' resources to aid Europe in reconstruction. The victors and the old enemy combined in power politics to bring pressure against us and finally to repudiate even the money we loaned for their own rebuilding. In the meantime, they have accumulated balances and assets in this country several times the amount of the payments.

When our agriculture wallowed in misery from its over-expansion in the war to furnish them food supplies, did they not, all of them, rush to other markets, impose quotas that favored nations which had given them no aid?

We have never complained. We do not now. We realize the nature of selfishness in all nations. We realize too well the age-old malign forces of Europe. We realize the poverty and despair under which these people live. But the voice of experience calls to us never again to assume that nations do not put their own interests first.

THE WAY IN WHICH WARS END

There is another experience that Europe has demonstrated from the Great War and its aftermath which becomes important at this moment. We are again told that unless we join in, western civilization may be destroyed and we will be the next victim. Therefore, eventually, why not now? That is propaganda to condition the American mind for entry into this war.

Aside from the fact that Britain and France with their empires can defend themselves, if they stay on the defense, great wars do not end that way.

Great wars often enough end in peace before either side is the victor. When one side is the victor in modern wars it is because the other side has become exhausted. At that moment the victors are but one lap behind in the race of exhaustion.

Neither at the armistice in 1919 nor at the end of any other war were the victors or the vanquished ready for or desirous of starting another war. In other words not even the victor is going to pounce upon a powerful armed neutral. Especially they do not attack 130,000,000 people 3000 miles overseas, who have a capacity of 10,000,000 soldiers and 25,000 airplanes.

Moreover, there are other factors that enter at the end of any great war. The victors want indemnities and possessions. Indemnities can be paid only from the productivity of a people. Nations cannot be made to work by force. They have to be given hope. That means the national independence of the enemy must be preserved by the victor. World trade has to be restored. In other words, even victors have to return to the paths of peace if they wish to restore their own exhaustion.

Beyond all this, when all great wars end, all the peoples take out their sufferings upon their leaders, either by putting them out of office or by revolution. And therefore the whole setting changes.

The voice of experience says we should discard these forebodings about being the next victim. . . .

A FEW OTHER CONSIDERATIONS FROM EXPERIENCE

What is the menace today that calls us again to join in European war? We are told we must join in a 'holy war' against ideologies that threaten the world.

But our citizens who advocate an American Don Quixote role of tilting at the windmills of lawless and obnoxious ideologies have certain elements of inconsistency. Their emotions have been concentrated on the ideologies of Nazi-ism and its softer manifestations of Fascism. They studiously overlooked Communism until the Hitler-Stalin pact.

During the whole of these twenty-odd years since Communism has become ascendant in Russia, from that base it has been subsidized to undermine democracies everywhere. Yet none of these abolitionists of ideologies had suggested that we go to war with Russia.

If we are going to clean up the noxious ideologies of the world, we will not have succeeded until we have also cleaned up Russia, as well as Germany and some 12 other totalitarian nations.

This experience with Russia proves still another thing. It is not true that we cannot somehow live at peace in the same world with an obnoxious ideology.

And here again must we listen to the voice of experience. You cannot defeat an idea or an ideology with military force. These can be educated out of people only by their own experience. Did the Great War extirpate the idea that might makes right? Did it really implant the noble ideals of peace, of cooperation, and of human liberty?

The voice of experience says America cannot correct the world every time it goes wrong. We should destroy our physical and moral strength in a decade if we set ourselves to police the conduct and ideas of the world. And our service to mankind would end.

SERVICE TO MANKIND

But today Europe is in agony. Our every instinct cries out to help in some way.

What is the greatest service that America can perform for Europe and mankind in this situation? I may repeat:

First. We can strengthen our Army and Navy to a point where no soldier dare land on the Western Hemisphere, irrespective of who wins the war in Europe. The building of that strength is the only warning that counts. It guarantees the peace of one-half the globe.

Second. We can put our own house in order. We can demonstrate that self-governing, free people can solve the problems imposed by the industrial revolution. We can restore employment and end its sufferings. We can build up humane measures of security, of increasing standards of living for all the people. We can wipe out of our midst the disintegrating forces of corruption and coercion of men.

Third. We can thus make a demonstration on this continent that true liberalism is not dead. We can hold alight to a crumbling world the lamp of liberty as the guide to regeneration. We can prove that the hope of humanity lies not in killing or regimenting men but in preserving them and in enlarging their lives.

Fourth. We can from our strength again heal many wounds of war. We can aid the starving, succor the distressed, and care for the innocent.

Fifth. We can aid those who sit at the peace table, not by entanglement but by counsel to mitigate malignance. We can, as President Wilson did in 1919, secure some justice, some freedom, some hope to the world.

We shall never be in a position to contribute even this small portion to the salvation of mankind if we ever become a participant in this war.

America, too, has a duty wholly to her own people. From them is coming a stern demand that we must not again sacrifice our youth for a useless hope. I know whereof I speak. My daily mail is heavy with their concern. Our young men are ready to die on our own soil for our own country, but they are defiant against their sacrifice for others' quarrels. Their mothers and fathers, who have skimped and denied themselves that their sons might be even better equipped to serve their country than they have been able to, are filled with anxiety lest the hope of their life service be lost. Our sympathies for the democracies will be drawn upon heavily in the days to come. Our duty to our sons is to hold reason in power over emotion. It is to hold the long vision of America's future. It is to keep out of these wars.

Herbert Hoover, *Further Addresses on the American Road, 1939–1940* (New York, 1940), pp. 139-57 (excerpts)

(b) *Charles A. Lindbergh: address to 'America First', New York City, April 22, 1941*

I shall discuss the war from a viewpoint which is primarily practical. It is not that I believe ideals are unimportant, even among the realities of war; but if a nation is to survive in a hostile world, its ideals must be backed by the hard logic of military practicability. If the outcome of war depended upon ideals alone, this would be a different world than it is today.

I know I will be severely criticized by the interventionists in America when I say we should not enter a war unless we have a reasonable chance of winning. That, they will claim, is far too materialistic a viewpoint. They will advance again the same arguments that were used to persuade France to declare war against Germany in 1939. But I do not believe that our American ideals, and our way of life, will gain through an unsuccessful war. And I know that the United States is not prepared to wage war in Europe successfully at this time. We are no better prepared today than France was when the interventionists in Europe persuaded her to attack the Siegfried Line.

I have said before, and I will say again, that I believe it will be a tragedy to the entire world if the British Empire collapses. That is one of the main reasons why I opposed this war before it was declared, and why I have constantly advocated a negotiated peace. I did not feel that England and France had a reasonable chance of winning. France has now been defeated; and, despite the propaganda and confusion of recent months, it is now obvious that England is losing the war. I believe this is realized even by the British Government. But they have one last desperate plan remaining. They hope that they may be able to persuade us to send another American Expeditionary Force to Europe, and to share with England militarily, as well as financially, the fiasco of this war.

I do not blame England for this hope, or for asking for our assistance. But we now know that she declared a war under circumstances which led to the defeat of every nation that sided with her from Poland to Greece. We know that in the desperation of war England promised to all those nations armed assistance that she could not send. We know that she misinformed them, as she has misinformed us, concerning her state of preparation, her military strength, and the progress of the war. . . .

It is not only our right, but is our obligation as American citizens to look at this war objectively and to weigh our chances for success if we should enter it. I have attempted to do this, especially from the standpoint of aviation; and I have been forced to the conclusion that we cannot win this war for England, regardless of how much assistance we extend.

I ask you to look at the map of Europe today and see if you can suggest any way in which we could win this war if we entered it. Suppose we had a large army in America, trained and equipped. Where would we send it to fight? The campaigns of the war show only too clearly how difficult it is to force a landing, or to maintain any army, on a hostile coast.

Suppose we took our Navy from the Pacific, and used it to convoy British shipping. That would not win the war for England. It would at best permit her to exist under the constant bombing of the German air fleet. Suppose we had an air force that we could send to Europe. Where could it operate? Some of our squadrons might be based in the British Isles; but it is physically impossible to base enough aircraft in the British Isles alone to equal in strength the aircraft that can be based on the Continent of Europe.

I have asked these questions on the supposition that we had in existence an Army and an air force large enough and well enough equipped to send to Europe; and that we would dare to remove our Navy from the Pacific. Even on this basis, I do not see how we could invade the Continent of Europe successfully as long as all of the Continent and most of Asia is under Axis domination. But the fact is that none of these suppositions are correct. We have only a one-ocean Navy. Our Army is still untrained and inadequately equipped for foreign war. Our air force is deplorably lacking in modern fighting planes.

When these facts are cited, the interventionists shout that we are defeatists, that we are undermining the principles of democracy, and that we are giving comfort to Germany by talking about our military weakness. But everything I mention here has been published in our newspapers, and in the reports of congressional hearings in Washington. Our military position is well known to the governments of Europe and Asia. Why, then, should it not be brought to the attention of our own people?

I say it is the interventionist in America, as it was in England and in France, who gives comfort to the enemy. I say it is they who are undermining the principles of democracy when they demand that we take a course to which more than 80 per cent of our citizens are opposed. I charge them with being the real defeatists, for their policy has led to the defeat of every country that followed their advice since this war began. There is no better way to give comfort to an enemy than to divide the people of a nation over the issue of foreign war. There is no shorter road to defeat than by entering a war with inadequate preparation. Every nation that has adopted the interventionist policy of depending on some one else for its own defense has met with nothing but defeat and failure. . . .

There are many such interventionists in America, but there are more people among us of a different type. That is why you and I are assembled here tonight. There is a policy open to this nation that will lead to success – a policy that leaves us free to follow our own way of life, and to develop our own civilization. It is not a new and untried idea. It was advocated by Washington. It was incorporated in the Monroe Doctrine. Under its guidance, the United States became the greatest nation in the world.

It is based upon the belief that the security of a nation lies in the strength and character of its own people. It recommends the maintenance of armed forces sufficient to defend this hemisphere from attack by any combination of foreign powers. It demands faith in an independent American destiny. This is the policy of the America First Committee today. It is a policy not of isolation, but of independence; not of defeat, but of courage. It is a policy that led this nation to success during the most trying years of our history, and it is a policy that will lead us to success again.

We have weakened ourselves for many months, and still worse, we have divided our own people by this dabbling in Europe's wars. While we should have been concentrating on American defense we have been forced to argue over foreign quarrels. We must turn our eyes and our faith back to our own country before it is too late. And when we do this, a different vista opens before us. Practically every difficulty we would face in invading Europe becomes an asset to us in defending America. Our enemy, and not we, would then have the problem of transporting millions of troops across the ocean and landing them on a hostile shore. They, and not we, would have to furnish the convoys to transport guns and trucks and munitions and fuel across three thousand miles of water. Our battleships and submarines would then be fighting close to their home bases. We would then do the bombing from the air and the torpedoing at sea. And if any part of an enemy convoy should ever pass our Navy and our air force, they would still be faced with the guns of our coast artillery and behind them the divisions of our Army.

The United States is better situated from a military standpoint than any other nation in the world. Even in our present condition of unpreparedness no foreign power is in a position to invade us today. If we concentrate on our own defenses and build the strength that this nation should maintain, no foreign army will ever attempt to land on American shores.

War is not inevitable for this country. Such a claim is defeatism in the true sense. No one can make us fight abroad unless we ourselves are willing to do so. No one will attempt to fight us here if we arm ourselves as a great nation should be armed. Over a hundred million people in this nation are opposed to entering the war. If the principles of democracy mean anything at all, that is reason enough for us to stay out. If we are forced into a war against the wishes of an overwhelming majority of our people, we will have proved democracy such a failure at home that there will be little use of fighting for it abroad.

The time has come when those of us who believe in an independent American destiny must band together and organize for strength. We have been led toward war by a minority of our people. This minority has power. It has influence. It has a loud voice. But it does not represent the American people. During the last several years I have traveled over this country from one end to the other. I have talked to many hundreds of men and women, and I have letters from tens of thousands more, who feel the same way as you and I. . . .

These people – the majority of hardworking American citizens, are with us. They are the true strength of our country. And they are beginning to realize, as you and I, that there are times when we must sacrifice our normal interests in life in order to insure the safety and the welfare of our nation.

Such a time has come. Such a crisis is here. That is why the America First Committee has been formed – to give voice to the people who have no newspaper, or newsreel, or radio station at their command; to the people who must do the paying, and the fighting, and the dying if this country enters the war.

Whether or not we do enter the war rests upon the shoulders of you in this audience, upon us here on this platform, upon meetings of this kind that are being held by Americans in every section of the United States today. It depends upon the action we take, and the courage we show at this time. If you believe in an independent destiny for America, if you believe that this country should not enter the war in Europe, we ask you to join the America First Committee in its stand. We ask you to share our faith in the ability of this nation to defend itself, to develop its own civilization, and to contribute to the progress of mankind in a more constructive and intelligent way than has yet been found by the warring nations of Europe. We need your support, and we need it now. The time to act is here.

New York Times, April 23, 1941

12 Politics and National Defence

Excerpt from the memoirs of Joseph Martin, Republican Minority Leader in the House of Representatives

In September 1940, Congress passed the Selective Service Act for one year. I voted for it. In the summer of 1941, while the United States was still precariously a nonbelligerent, the measure came back to us for renewal for another year and a half. This time a large number of Republicans in the House, frantic over the drift toward war, were violently opposed and put a great deal of heat on me to take a stand against extension. It was perfectly clear that if I defied this sentiment and, as leader, voted for extension, the Republican organization in the House would have been torn to pieces. Not only that, but my support of the administration bill might have alienated a substantial number of Republican voters.

Once more I was faced with my old problem of holding Republicans together. By this time I had learned that a leader sometimes has to go along with the majority of his group for a way in order to bring them around to his course in the end. If one is leading ninety soldiers and eighty want to walk in one direction and ten in the other, one has to make some concession or at least give the eighty a feeling that one is in sympathy with them. That, in sum, is what I did.

A case could be made against extension in the form in which it was proposed. In the original act Congress had in effect signed a contract with the men who had been drafted for one year, as was acknowledged by respected members on both sides of the aisle. I believed that the United States government should honor a contract, whether it involved a new post office or a soldier. One year was one year. This year would not have been up until November. In that month only about 13,000 would be eligible for discharge, which would not have crippled the armed services. By releasing these men Congress would be keeping its word. An added reassuring element in the situation was that as draftees were released, they could be recalled immediately as reserves to maintain the country's strength. I would not have been opposed to a new eighteen-month draft for new men; it was the adding of eighteen months to the service of those who would have been in a year already that bothered me.

Then another aspect presented itself. There was widespread public opposition to extension of the draft. So long as I could feel sure that the national security was not being jeopardized, as I did in this case, my position as Republican leader kept me on the alert for an issue that might yet funnel the winds into our sails and blow us back again to the commanding position the Republican Party had enjoyed in the 1920s. Where I could capitalize on an issue without harming the country, I did. The draft-extension bill was such a vehicle. Yet it had to be handled deftly lest public sentiment turn against us in the end. This might have happened if the Republicans had defeated the renewal of selective service. The country might have become alarmed, and that would have enabled Roosevelt to play upon the sense of shock to our detriment.

The course I followed, therefore, was to court such popular sentiment as we could attract by opposing the bill, yet at the same time make no great effort to defeat it. I regarded it as one of those fights in which one comes out stronger if one loses than if one wins. Thus, while as leader I voted against it myself, I hoped that it would pass. When certain Republican members who were in doubt came to me for advice, I would tell them, 'If I were you and it doesn't make any difference, follow your own preference on this'. I did not knock myself out trying to get their votes.

When the voting began, I was taken aback by the large number of Democrats who, under pressure from home, were lining up with Republicans against the bill. As we neared the end of the roll call, with sixty-five Democrats voting against Roosevelt, I had the sinking feeling that I might have made a fatal miscalculation. Contrary to my wishes, the bill might be defeated after all.

Finally, by a hair's breadth, it was passed 203 to 202. If I had wished, I could have got that one vote; when a leader comes that close he can always obtain an extra vote. But that was not my strategy. We lost, but won. Selective service had been extended, but the Republicans had made a record of keeping faith with the men who had been drafted for one year.

Joe Martin, *My First Fifty Years in Politics* (New York, 1960), pp. 96-8

V

FOREIGN POLICY AND GLOBAL WAR, 1941-5

Once America became a belligerent, the horizons of American policy became infinite. As Roosevelt once confided to Averell Harriman, 'You naturally understand that in this global war there is literally no question, political or military, in which the United States is not interested.' The documents in this chapter, a small sample from a vast sea of materials, suggest both the sweep and the principal thrusts of wartime policies.

President Roosevelt had, broadly speaking, three overriding goals: he sought total victory over the Axis at the earliest possible moment; he intended to replace the defunct League of Nations with a new international organisation; and, above all, he wanted to preserve the 'grand alliance' of Britain, Russia, and the United States not only as the instrument for victory but also as the nucleus around which the post-war international system would revolve.

Total victory was symbolised by the controversial policy of 'Unconditional Surrender', an objective first publicly announced (but never fully defined) at a brief press conference following the Casablanca Conference of January, 1943 (1).

Throughout the war years American foreign policy was the policy of Franklin D. Roosevelt. He was his own Secretary of State, and foreign affairs were personalised in the hands of the President to an even greater extent than in the days of Wilson. The relationship between the United States and Great Britain – more specifically, the relationship between Roosevelt and Churchill – was by far the closest and most harmonious. But beneath their wartime friendship lay important differences, not the least of which was FDR's suspicion of British colonial policies. He was firmly convinced that with victory the old British (and for that matter, French and Dutch) colonial systems should not be restored. Illustrative of Roosevelt's sentiments was his gratuitous advice to Churchill on the proper way to handle the movement for Indian independence. In a message to Churchill in 1942 Roosevelt, with something less than his customary political wisdom, urged Britain to build her Indian policy on the American model of the years from 1783 to 1789 (2)!

Maintaining the grand alliance called, so Roosevelt believed, for special attention to the Soviet Union and an unremitting effort to gain Stalin to the cause of post-war international co-operation. FDR was buoyantly confident that Stalin could be won over with time and patience. Whether his Russian policy was based upon *naïveté* about Communism or, just possibly, upon a prescient vision of the appalling consequences of failure to secure Russian co-operation, the nature of Roosevelt's approach to Stalin is clearly evident in his wartime discussions with the Soviet leader, especially in his extended talk with Stalin at the Teheran conference in November 1943 (**3**). It was at this meeting that Roosevelt first concluded that his efforts were beginning to succeed.

Roosevelt was long hesitant to sponsor a new League of Nations but eventually became the ardent advocate of what emerged as the United Nations. Of greater importance, however, was the sea change in basic American attitudes about the relationship of the United States to the world. Virtually all segments of American opinion came to agree that there must be a new international organisation, that America must participate in it, and that there must be no repetition of the Wilsonian debacle. The new attitude in Congress revealed itself in the Connally Resolution of November 1943 which committed the Senate to American membership in a post-war international organisation (**4** (**a**)). Symbolic of the change was the conversion of Senator Arthur Vandenberg of Michigan, once a leader of the hard-core isolationist wing of the Republican party. His speech in the Senate early in 1945 showed that the Republicans would not play the same rôle that they had played under Lodge in 1919 and were also prepared to adopt a bipartisan approach to foreign policy (**4** (**b**)).

Nevertheless, the change in American attitudes did not occur spontaneously. Many private and semi-public organisations were active in the movement for internationalism. The Protestant churches, for example, enlisted many shades of religious opinion on their Commission on a Just and Durable Peace, a group chaired by the New York lawyer and future Secretary of State, John Foster Dulles. The Commission's 'Six Pillars of Peace' not only stated the case for internationalism but also expressed the underlying idealism, hopes and expectations of those Americans who believed that World War II could usher in a new and peaceful world (**4** (**c**)).

Roosevelt cherished fond hopes that China under Chiang kai-shek would be accepted as one of the Big Four and eventually become the stabilising force in the Far East after the war. But the Chinese-American relationship was always sorely troubled. General Joseph Stilwell, dispatched to China to serve as Chiang's chief-of-staff, became involved in bitter disputes with the Nationalist leader (**5** (**a**)). Various State Department documents attest to the disarray into which Chinese-American relations soon fell (**5** (**b**), **5** (**c**)). Though Roosevelt himself never really changed his mind about Chiang or China's potential and, though the American public knew virtually nothing of the rancorous wartime disagreements, the Stilwell episode sowed the first seeds of eventual American disillusionment with Nationalist China and was an ominous indicator of the 'China problem' that would develop after 1945.

In February of 1945 the Allied leaders met at Yalta. Roosevelt was convinced that his goal of post-war co-operation with the Soviet Union had been achieved by the agreements reached at the Crimean conference. His report to Congress – indeed, his last major speech before his sudden death six weeks later – attests to that belief as well as to American expectations on the eve of victory (**6 (a)**). Whether FDR was 'disabused', in the few remaining weeks of his life, whether he was on the verge of changing his policies – these are controversial questions which, in the absence of definitive evidence, will long remain so. Certainly the President's last messages to Churchill do suggest a growing doubt about Soviet intentions, but they also manifest a desire to avoid any direct confrontation (**6 (b)**).

World War II ended with the cataclysmic destruction of two Japanese cities. On August 6, 1945, after the bombing of Hiroshima, President Truman announced the opening of the atomic age (**7 (a)**). But the bomb did not simply end the war; rather it opened up vast new international political problems. Should America share the bomb? Should she attempt to keep the secret of the atom to herself? Should the fearsome power of the bomb be used to coerce the Russians into accepting an American design for international order? The debate on the atomic bomb and its international implications was opened. Secretary Stimson's proposal – which came to naught – illustrates not only that these issues were immediately posed but also that atomic energy had created vast new international problems (**7 (b)**).

1 Unconditional Surrender

Statement of President Roosevelt at the Casablanca Conference, Jaunuary 24, 1943

. . . Another point. I think we have all had it in our hearts and our heads before, but I don't think that it has ever been put down on paper by the Prime Minister and myself, and that is the determination that peace can come to the world only by the total elimination of German and Japanese war power.

Some of you Britishers know the old story – we had a General called U. S. Grant. His name was Ulysses Simpson Grant, but in my, and the Prime Minister's, early days he was called 'Unconditional Surrender' Grant. The elimination of German, Japanese, and Italian war power means the unconditional surrender by Germany, Italy, and Japan. That means a reasonable assurance of future world peace. It does not mean the destruction of the population of Germany, Italy, or Japan, but it does mean the destruction of the philosophies in those countries which are based on conquest and the subjugation of other people. . . .

Public Papers and Addresses of Franklin D. Roosevelt (New York, 1950), Vol. 12, p. 39

2 Roosevelt and Colonialism: India

President Roosevelt to Prime Minister Churchill, March 10, 1942

I have given much thought to the problem of India and I am grateful that you have kept me in touch with it.

As you can well realize, I have felt much diffidence in making any suggestions, and it is a subject which, of course, all of you good people know far more about than I do.

I have tried to approach the problem from the point of view of history and with a hope that the injection of a new thought to be used in India might be of assistance to you.

That is why I go back to the inception of the Government of the United States. During the Revolution, from 1775 to 1783, the British Colonies set themselves up as Thirteen States, each one under a different form of government, although each one assumed individual sovereignty. While the war lasted there was great confusion between these separate sovereignties, and the only two connecting links were the Continental Congress (a body of ill-defined powers and large inefficiencies) and second the Continental Army which was rather badly maintained by the Thirteen States. In 1783, at the end of the war, it was clear that the new responsibilities of the thirteen sovereignties could not be welded into a Federal Union because the experiment was still in the making and any effort to arrive at a final framework would have come to naught.

Therefore, the thirteen sovereignties joined in the Articles of Confederation, an obvious stop-gap government, to remain in effect only until such time as experience and trial and error could bring about a permanent union. The thirteen sovereignties, from 1783 to 1789, proved, through lack of a Federal power, that they would soon fly apart into separate nations. In 1787 a Constitutional Convention was held with only twenty-five or thirty active participants, representing all of the States. They met, not as a Parliament, but as a small group of sincere patriots, with the sole objective of establishing a Federal Government. The discussion was recorded but the meetings were not held before an audience. The present Constitution of the United States resulted and soon received the assent of two-thirds of the States.

It is merely a thought of mine to suggest the setting up of what might be called a temporary government in India, headed by a small representative group, covering different castes, occupations, religions and geographies – this group to be recognized as a temporary Dominion Government. It would, of course, represent existing governments of the British Provinces and would also represent the Council of Princes.

But my principal thought is that it would be charged with setting up a body to consider a more permanent government for the whole country – this consideration to be extended over a period of five or six years or at least until a year after the end of the war.

I suppose that this Central Temporary governing group, speaking for the new Dominion, would have certain executive and administrative powers over public services, such as finances, railways, telegraphs and other things which we call public services.

Perhaps the analogy of some such method to the travails and problems of the United States from 1783 to 1789 might give a new slant in India itself, and it might cause the people there to forget hard feelings, to become more loyal to the British Empire, and to stress the danger of Japanese domination, together with the advantage of peaceful evolution as against chaotic revolution.

Such a move is strictly in line with the world changes of the past half century and with the democratic processes of all who are fighting Nazism.

I hope that whatever you do the move will be made from London and that there should be no criticism in India that it is being made grudgingly or by compulsion.

For the love of Heaven don't bring me into this, though I do want to be of help. It is, strictly speaking, none of my business, except insofar as it is a part and parcel of the successful fight that you and I are making.

Papers relating to the Foreign Relations of the United States, 1942, Vol. I (Washington, 1960), pp. 615–16

3 The President and the Marshal

Conversations between President Roosevelt and Marshal Stalin at the Teheran Conference, November 2, 1943

THE PRESIDENT then said he had a great many other matters relating to the future of the world which he would like to talk over informally with the Marshal and obtain his view on them. He said that he hoped to discuss some of them before they left Teheran. He said that he was willing to discuss any subject military or political which the Marshal desired.

MARSHAL STALIN replied there was nothing to prevent them from discussing anything they wished.

THE PRESIDENT then said the question of a post war organization to preserve peace had not been fully explained and dealt with and he would like to discuss with the Marshal the prospect of some organization based on the United Nations.

THE PRESIDENT then outlined the following general plan:

(1) There would be a large organization composed of some 35 members of the United Nations which would meet periodically at different places, discuss and make recommendations to a smaller body.

MARSHAL STALIN inquired whether this organization was to be world-wide or European, to which the President replied, world-wide.

THE PRESIDENT continued that there would be set up an executive committee composed of the Soviet Union, the United States, United Kingdom and China, together with two additional European states, one South American, one Near East, one Far Eastern country, and one British Dominion. He mentioned that Mr. Churchill did not like this proposal for the reason that the British Empire only had two votes. This Executive Committee would deal with all non-military questions such as agriculture, food, health, and economic questions, as well as the setting up of an International Committee. This Committee would likewise meet in various places.

MARSHAL STALIN inquired whether this body would have the right to make decisions binding on the nations of the world.

THE PRESIDENT replied, yes and no. It could make recommendations for settling disputes with the hope that the nations concerned would be guided thereby, but that, for example, he did not believe the Congress of the United States would accept as binding a decision of such a body. THE PRESIDENT then turned to the third organization which he termed 'The Four Policemen', namely, the Soviet Union, United States, Great Britain, and China. This organization would have the power to deal immediately with any threat to the peace and any sudden emergency which requires this action. He went on to say that in 1935, when Italy attacked Ethiopia, the only machinery in existence was the League of Nations. He personally had begged France to close the Suez Canal, but they instead referred it to the League which disputed the question and in the end did nothing. The result was that the Italian Armies went through the Suez Canal and destroyed Ethiopia. THE PRESIDENT pointed out that had the machinery of the

Four Policemen, which he had in mind, been in existence, it would have been possible to close the Suez Canal. THE PRESIDENT then summarized briefly the idea that he had in mind.

MARSHAL STALIN said that he did not think that the small nations of Europe would like the organization composed of the Four Policemen. He said, for example, that a European state would probably resent China having the right to apply certain machinery to it. And in any event, he did not think China would be very powerful at the end of the war. He suggested as a possible alternative, the creation of a European or a Far Eastern Committee and a European or a Worldwide organization. He said that in the European Commission there would be the United States, Great Britain, the Soviet Union and possibly one other European state.

THE PRESIDENT said that the idea just expressed by Marshal Stalin was somewhat similar to Mr. Churchill's idea of a Regional Committee, one for Europe, one for the Far East, and one for the Americas. Mr. Churchill had also suggested that the United States be a member of the European Commission, but he doubted if the United States Congress would agree to the United States' participation in an exclusively European Committee which might be able to force the dispatch of American troops to Europe.

THE PRESIDENT added that it would take a terrible crisis such as at present before Congress would ever agree to that step.

MARSHAL STALIN pointed out that the world organization suggested by the President, and in particular the Four Policemen, might also require the sending of American troops to Europe.

THE PRESIDENT pointed out that he had only envisaged the sending of American planes and ships to Europe, and that England and the Soviet Union would have to handle the land armies in the event of any future threat to the peace. He went on to say that if the Japanese had not attacked the United States he doubted very much if it would have been possible to send any American forces to Europe. THE PRESIDENT added that he saw two methods of dealing with possible threats to the peace. In one case if the threat arose from a revolution or developments in a small country, it might be possible to apply the quarantine method, closing the frontiers of the countries in question and imposing embargoes. In the second case, if the threat was more serious, the four powers, acting as policemen, would send an ultimatum to the nation in question and if refused, [it] would result in the immediate bombardment and possible invasion of that country.

MARSHAL STALIN said that yesterday he had discussed the question of safeguarding against Germany with Mr. Churchill and found him optimistic on the subject in that Mr. Churchill believed that Germany would not rise again. He, Stalin, personally thought that unless prevented, Germany would completely recovery [*recover*] within 15 to 20 years, and that therefore we must have something more serious than the type of organization proposed by the President. He pointed out that the first German aggression had occurred in 1870 and then 42 [*44*] years later in the 1st World War, whereas only 21 years elapsed between the end of the last war and the beginning of the present. He added that he did not believe the period between the revival of German strength would be any longer in the future and therefore he did not consider the organizations outlined by the President were enough.

He went on to say that what was needed was the control of certain strong physical points either within Germany along German borders, or even farther away, to insure that Germany would not embark on another course of aggression. He mentioned specifically Dakar as one of those points. He added that the same method should be applied in the case of Japan and that the islands in the vicinity of Japan should remain under strong control to prevent Japan's embarking on a course of aggression.

He stated that any commission or body which was set up to preserve peace should have the right to not only make decisions but to occupy such strong points against Germany and Japan.

THE PRESIDENT said that he agreed 100% with Marshal Stalin.

MARSHAL STALIN then stated he still was dubious about the question of Chinese participation.

THE PRESIDENT replied that he had insisted on the participation of China in the 4 Power Declaration at Moscow not because he did not realize the weakness of China at present, but he was thinking farther into the future and that after all China was a nation of 400 million people, and it was better to have them as friends rather than as a potential source of trouble.

THE PRESIDENT, reverting to Marshal Stalin's statements as to the ease of converting factories, said that a strong and effective world organization of the 4 Powers could move swiftly when the first signs arose of the beginning of the conversion of such factories for warlike purposes.

MARSHAL STALIN replied that the Germans had shown great ability to conceal such beginnings.

THE PRESIDENT accepted Marshal Stalin's remark. He again expressed his agreement with Marshal Stalin that strategic positions in the world should be at the disposal of some world organization to prevent a revival of German and Japanese aggression.

Papers Relating to the Foreign Relations of the United States: The Conferences at Cairo and Teheran (Washington, 1963), pp. 530–3

4 The Movement for Internationalism

(a) *The Connally Resolution: Senate Resolution 192, 78th Congress, November 5, 1943*

Resolved, That the war against all our enemies be waged until complete victory is achieved.

That the United States cooperate with its comrades-in-arms in securing a just and honorable peace.

That the United States, acting through its constitutional processes, join with free and sovereign nations in the establishment and maintenance of international authority with power to prevent aggression and to preserve the peace of the world.

That the Senate recognizes the necessity of there being established at the earliest practicable date a general international organization, based on the principle of the sovereign equality of all peace-loving states, and open to membership by all such states, large and small, for the maintenance of international peace and security.

That, pursuant to the Constitution of the United States, any treaty made to effect the purposes of this resolution, on behalf of the Government of the United States with any other nation or any association of nations, shall be made only by and with the advice and consent of the Senate of the United States, provided two-thirds of the Senators present concur.

Senate Foreign Relations Committee, *A Decade of American Foreign Policy, 1941–1949* (Washington, 1950), p. 14 (81st Congress, 1st Session, Senate Document 123) (hereafter abbreviated as *A Decade of American Foreign Policy*)

(b) *The Conversion of an Isolationist: Excerpts from speech by Senator Arthur Vandenberg of Michigan, United States Senate, January 10, 1945*

I hasten to make my own personal viewpoint clear. I have always been frankly one of those who has believed in our own self-reliance. I still believe that we can never again – regardless of collaborations – allow our national defense to deteriorate to anything like a point of impotence. But I do not believe that any nation hereafter can immunize itself by its own exclusive action. Since Pearl Harbor, World War II has put the gory science of mass murder into new and sinister perspective. Our oceans have ceased to be moats which automatically protect our ramparts. Flesh and blood now compete unequally with winged steel. War has become an all-consuming juggernaut. If World War III ever unhappily arrives, it will open new laboratories of death too horrible to contemplate. I propose to do everything within my power to keep those laboratories closed for keeps.

I want maximum American cooperation, consistent with legitimate American self-interest, with constitutional process and with collateral events which warrant it, to make the basic idea of Dumbarton Oaks succeed. I want a new dignity and a new authority for international law.

I think American self-interest requires it. But, Mr. President, this also requires whole-hearted reciprocity. In honest candor, I think we should tell other nations that this glorious thing we contemplate is not and cannot be one-sided. I think we must say again that unshared idealism is a menace which we could not undertake to underwrite in the post-war world. . . .

The real question always becomes just this: Where does real self-interest lie? Here, Mr. President, we reach the core of the immediate problem. Without remotely wanting to be invidious, I use one of many available examples. I would not presume, even under these circumstances, to use it except that it ultimately involves us. Russia's unilateral plan appears to contemplate the engulfment, directly or indirectly, of a surrounding circle of buffer states, contrary to our conception of what we thought we were fighting for in respect to the rights of small nations and a just peace. Russia's announced reason is her insistent purpose never again to be at the mercy of another German tyranny. That is a perfectly understandable reason. The alternative is collective security. . . . Which is better in the long view, from a purely selfish Russian standpoint: To forcefully surround herself with a cordon of unwillingly controlled or partitioned states, thus affronting the opinions of mankind . . . or to win the priceless asset of world confidence in her by embracing the alternative, namely, full and whole-hearted cooperation with and reliance on a vital international organization. . . . Well – at that point, Russia, or others like her, in equally honest candor has a perfect right to reply, 'Where is there any such alternative reliance until we know what the United States will do?' . . .

I propose that we meet this problem conclusively and at once. There is no reason to wait. America has this same self-interest in permanently, conclusively and effectively disarming Germany and Japan. . . . It should be handled as this present war is handled. There should be no more need to refer any such action [use of force to keep the Axis disarmed] back to Congress than that Congress should expect to pass upon battle plans today. The Commander-in-Chief should have instant power to act and he should act. I know of no reason why a hard-and-fast treaty between the major allies should not be signed today to achieve this dependable end. We need not await the determination of our other postwar relationships. This problem – this menace – stands apart by itself . . . I respectfully urge that we meet this problem now.

Congressional Record, 79th Congress, 1st Session, Senate, January 10, 1945, pp. 164–8

(c) *'A Just and Durable Peace': Statement of Political Propositions formulated by the Commission on a Just and Durable Peace of the Federal Council of the Churches of Christ in America, March 1943* (*Chairman: John Foster Dulles*)

The American people again find themselves in an era of critical decision. It must now be determined, this time in worldwide terms, whether men are capable of establishing good government from reflection and choice, or whether they will continue to be buffeted about by force and by accident. Now, as before, it is reserved to the people of this country to play a decisive role. Now, more than ever, a wrong choice of the part we shall act will involve us in the general misfortune of mankind. . . .

Military peril has dramatized, for all to see, the need for international cooperation. But as military victory becomes more certain and draws more near, that need will be less obvious. As we come to grips with the appalling moral, social and material aftermaths of Axis rule, transitory issues will arise to perplex and divide the United Nations. These may loom large and obscure the fundamental and incline us to relapse into reliance only upon our own strength. Thus, if our nation does not make the right choice soon, it may never be made in our time. . . .

We have stated our Propositions in simple and minimum terms. We recognize that as so stated there is much latitude as to their form and detailed content and as to the timing of their full realization. These matters are important and their determination will involve much honest differences of opinion which, ultimately, must be reconciled. But the Propositions, as stated by us, serve to force the initial and vital decision on the direction in which this nation will move. They force that decision in relation to six major areas within which the factual interdependence of the world has become such as to require political mechanism for cooperative action. If the six Propositions we enunciate become an official program of this nation, we will be committed to move, by definitive steps, to bring ourselves into an ordered relationship with others. Only if the nations join to do this can we escape chaos and recurrent war. Only if the United States assumes a leadership can it be done now. For we, more than any other nation, have the capacity to influence decisively the shaping of world events. If the future is to be other than a repetition of the past, the United States must accept a responsibility for constructive action commensurate with its power and opportunity.

STATEMENT OF POLITICAL PROPOSITIONS

I

The peace must provide the political framework for a continuing collaboration of the United Nations and, in due course, of neutral and enemy nations.

II

The peace must make provision for bringing within the scope of international agreement those economic and financial acts of national governments which have widespread international repercussions.

III

The peace must make provision for an organization to adapt the treaty structure of the world to changing underlying conditions.

IV

The peace must proclaim the goal of autonomy for subject peoples, and it must establish international organization to assure and to supervise the realization of that end.

V

The peace must establish procedures for controlling military establishments everywhere.

VI

The peace must establish in principle, and seek to achieve in practice, the right of individuals everywhere to religious and intellectual liberty.

The Papers of John Foster Dulles (Princeton University Library, Princeton, N.J.)

5 Troubled Relations with China

(a) *Vinegar Joe and the Peanut: Excerpt from the diaries of General Joseph Stilwell, July–September 1944*

SOLUTION IN CHINA [Probably July 1944] The cure for China's trouble is the elimination of Chiang K'ai-shek. The only thing that keeps the country split is his fear of losing control. He hates the Reds and will not take any chances on giving them a toehold in the government. The result is that each side watches the other and neither gives a damn about the war [against Japan]. If this condition persists, China will have civil war immediately after Japan is out. If Russia enters the war before a united front is formed in China, the Reds, being immediately accessible, will naturally gravitate to Russia's influence and control. The condition will directly affect the relations between Russia and China, and therefore indirectly those between Russia and U.S.

If we do not take action, our prestige in China will suffer seriously. China will contribute nothing to our effort against Japan, and the seeds will be planted for chaos in China after the war. . . .

SEPTEMBER 19 Mark this day in red on the calendar of life. At long, at very long last, F.D.R. has finally spoken plain words, and plenty of them, with a firecracker in every sentence. 'Get busy or else.' A hot firecracker. I handed this bundle of paprika to the Peanut and then sank back with a sigh.[1] The harpoon hit the little bugger right in the solar plexus, and went right through him. It was a clean hit, but beyond turning green and losing the power of speech, he did not bat an eye. He just said to me, 'I understand'. And sat in silence, jiggling one foot. We are now a long way from the 'tribal chieftain' bawling out. *Two long years lost*, but at least F.D.R.'s eyes have been opened and he has thrown a good hefty punch.

[1] Stilwell refers to a sharply worded demand by FDR that Chiang reform his government; the telegram arrived at Stilwell's headquarters on September 19th, and the American general was ordered to deliver it personally to Chiang. 'The Peanut' is, of course, Chiang – the term that 'Vinegar Joe' Stilwell used throughout his diary.

. . . It has taken two and a half years for the Big Boys to see the light, but it dawned finally and I played the avenging angel.

> I've waited long for vengeance—
> At last I've had my chance.
> I've looked the Peanut in the eye
> And kicked him in the pants.
>
> The old harpoon was ready
> With aim and timing true,
> I sank it to the handle,
> And stung him through and through.
>
> The little bastard shivered,
> And lost the power of speech.
> His face turned green and quivered
> As he struggled not to screech.
>
> For all my weary battles,
> For all my hours of woe,
> At last I've had my innings
> And laid the Peanut low.
>
> I know I've still to suffer,
> And run a weary race,
> But oh! the blessed pleasure!
> I've wrecked the Peanut's face.

'Rejoice with me and be exceeding glad, for lo! we have prevailed over the Philistine and bowed his head in the dust, and his heart is heavy.'

The dope is that after I left the screaming [Chiang's] began and lasted into the night.

Joseph W. Stilwell, *The Stilwell Papers* (New York, 1948), pp. 255, 263-4

(b) *Message from Ambassador Gauss to Secretary of State Hull, September 28, 1944*

My Dear Mr. Secretary: With reference to the mission to China of Mr. Donald Nelson and Major General Patrick J. Hurley, personal representatives of the President, I enclose for your information copies of the agenda prepared by these gentlemen for their discussions with Generalissimo Chiang Kai-shek. . . .

With reference to the Hurley agenda, I am informed that while Generalissimo Chiang was at first agreeable to the appointment of General Stilwell as field commander in China, certain recent developments have served to revive the friction between Stilwell and Chiang and the latter is now unwilling to accept the Stilwell appointment. While I have long known of the Chiang-Stilwell feud, which dates back several years, I have not known its details. I have regretted the lack of harmony and understanding between the Generalissimo and the American commander, but neither of them has at any time informed me of their difficulties. Both Dr. Soong, the Foreign Minister, who has been participating in the Chiang-Hurley conversations, and General Hurley himself apparently consider that the present break between the Generalissimo and Stilwell is irreparable and final. Apparently consideration is now being given to the selection of some other American officer as Allied field commander in China. The post will require an officer of great ability, patience and tact; and one not unfamiliar with the Oriental mind. . . .

Papers relating to the Foreign Relations of the United States, 1944, China (Washington, 1967), pp. 256–7, 259–60.

(c) *Memorandum by the Chief of the Division of Chinese Affairs, John Vincent, to the Director of the Office of Far Eastern Affairs, Joseph C. Grew, October 2, 1946*

Mr. Grew: This morning . . . I called on Mr. Donald Nelson. We discussed present and postwar economic problems in China for about an hour. Mr. Nelson was quite outspoken and gave us a very interesting account of his visit. Mr. Sumner is preparing a memorandum based on the conversation.

At the conclusion of the conference, Mr. Nelson detained me for a few minutes to discuss the political situation. He said with great emphasis that our relations with China were bad – 'very bad'. The attitude of our Army in China is primarily responsible for this situation. United States Army personnel in general adopts an unsympathetic, even antagonistic, attitude toward China. Relations between Chiang Kai-shek and General Stilwell are most unfortunate. Chiang does not like Stilwell and Stilwell does not have the personality successfully to deal with Chiang. Consequently there is continuous friction and irritation. Mr. Nelson mentioned one particular instance which occurred while he was in Chungking as illustrative of how Stilwell should not handle Chiang.

I asked about General Hurley. Mr. Nelson said that Hurley was early convinced of the futility of his mission and had planned to come home with him but had been dissuaded from doing so by General Stilwell. Mr. Nelson does not anticipate that Hurley will be able to accomplish much.

Mr. Nelson spoke well of Ambassador Gauss and of the Embassy staff in general but he said that relations between Chiang Kai-shek and the Ambassador were not good. The Ambassador's personality is against him in dealing with Chiang and Chiang feels that he is antagonistic. This situation, Mr. Nelson says, has been made worse by the Ambassador's close relations with T. V. Soong. T. V. Soong is still in the 'dog house' and therefore the closeness of Gauss and 'T.V.' is not conducive to good working relations between Chiang and Gauss.

Papers relating to the Foreign Relations of the United States, 1944, China (Washington, 1967), pp. 256–7, 259–60

6 Yalta: The Promise and the Doubt

(a) *Address of President Roosevelt to a Joint Session of Congress Reporting on the Yalta Conference, March 1, 1945*

I hope that you will pardon me for this unusual posture of sitting down during the presentation of what I want to say, but I know that you will realize that it makes it a lot easier for me not to have to carry about ten pounds of steel around on the bottom of my legs; and also because of the fact that I have just completed a fourteen-thousand-mile trip.

First of all, I want to say, it is good to be home.

It has been a long journey. I hope you will also agree that it has been, so far, a fruitful one.

Speaking in all frankness, the question of whether it is entirely fruitful or not lies to a great extent in your hands. For unless you here in the halls of the American Congress – with the support of the American people – concur in the general conclusions reached at Yalta, and give them your active support, the meeting will not have produced lasting results. . . .

I come from the Crimea Conference with a firm belief that we have made a good start on the road to a world of peace.

There were two main purposes in this Crimea Conference. The first was to bring defeat to Germany with the greatest possible speed, and the smallest possible loss of Allied men. That purpose is now being carried out in great force. The German Army, and the German people, are feeling the ever-increasing might of our fighting men and of the Allied armies. Every hour gives us added pride in the heroic advance of our troops in Germany – on German soil – toward a meeting with the gallant Red Army.

The second purpose was to continue to build the foundation for an international accord that would bring order and security after the chaos of the war, that would give some assurance of lasting peace among the Nations of the world. . . .

At the Crimea Conference, however, the time had come for getting down to specific cases in the political field.

There was on all sides at this Conference an enthusiastic effort to reach an agreement. Since the time of Teheran, a year ago, there had developed among all of us a – what shall I call it? – a greater facility in negotiating with each other, that augurs well for the peace of the world. We know each other better.

I have never for an instant wavered in my belief that an agreement to insure world peace and security can be reached. . . .

When we met at Yalta, in addition to laying our strategic and tactical plans for the complete and final military victory over Germany, there were other problems of vital political consequence.

For instance, first, there were the problems of the occupation and control of Germany – after victory – the complete destruction of her military power, and the assurance that neither the Nazis nor Prussian militarism could again be revived to threaten the peace and the civilization of the world.

Second – again for example – there was the settlement of the few differences that remained among us with respect to the International Security Organization after the Dumbarton Oaks Conference. As you remember, at that time, I said that we had agreed ninety percent. Well, that's a pretty good percentage. I think the other ten percent was ironed out at Yalta.

Third, there were the general political and economic problems common to all of the areas which had been or would be liberated from the Nazi yoke. This is a very special problem. We over here find it difficult to understand the ramifications of many of these problems in foreign lands, but we are trying to.

Fourth, there were the special problems created by a few instances such as Poland and Yugoslavia.

Days were spent in discussing these momentous matters and we argued freely and frankly across the table. But at the end, on every point, unanimous agreement was reached. And more important even than the agreement of words, I may say we achieved a unity of thought and a way of getting along together.

Of course, we know that it was Hitler's hope – and the German war lords – that we would not agree – that some slight crack might appear in the solid wall of Allied unity, a crack that would give him and his fellow gangsters one last hope of escaping their just doom. That is the objective for which his propaganda machine has been working for many months.

But Hitler has failed.

Never before have the major Allies been more closely united – not only in their war aims but also in their peace aims. And they are determined to continue to be united with each other – and with all peace-loving Nations – so that the ideal of lasting peace will become a reality. . . .

The German people, as well as the German soldiers must realize that the sooner they give up and surrender by groups or as individuals, the sooner their present agony will be over. They must realize that only with complete surrender can they begin to reestablish themselves as people whom the world might accept as decent neighbors.

We made it clear again at Yalta, and I now repeat that unconditional surrender does not mean the destruction or enslavement of the German people. The Nazi leaders have deliberately withheld that part of the Yalta declaration from the German press and radio. They seek to convince the people of Germany that the Yalta declaration does mean slavery and destruction for them – they are working at it day and night for that is how the Nazis hope to save their own skins, and deceive their people into continued and useless resistance.

We did, however, make it clear at the Conference just what unconditional surrender does mean for Germany.

It means the temporary control of Germany by Great Britain, Russia, France, and the United States. Each of these Nations will occupy and control a separate zone of Germany – and the administration of the four zones will be coordinated in Berlin by a Control Council composed of representatives of the four Nations.

Unconditional surrender means something else. It means the end of Nazism. It means the end of the Nazi Party – and of all its barbaric laws and institutions.

It means the termination of all militaristic influence in the public, private, and cultural life of Germany.

It means for the Nazi war criminals a punishment that is speedy and just – and severe.

It means the complete disarmament of Germany; the destruction of its militarism and its military equipment; the end of its production of armament; the dispersal of all its armed forces; the permanent dismemberment of the German General Staff which has so often shattered the peace of the world.

It means that Germany will have to make reparations in kind for the damage which has been done to the innocent victims of its aggression.

By compelling reparations in kind – in plants, in machinery, in rolling stock, and in raw materials – we shall avoid the mistake that we and other Nations made after the last war, the demanding of reparations in the form of money which Germany could never pay.

We do not want the German people to starve, or to become a burden on the rest of the world.

Our objective in handling Germany is simple – it is to secure the peace of the rest of the world now and in the future. Too much experience has shown that that objective is impossible if Germany is allowed to retain any ability to wage aggressive warfare.

These objectives will not hurt the German people. On the contrary, they will protect them from a repetition of the fate which the General Staff and Kaiserism imposed on them before, and which Hitlerism is now imposing upon them again a hundredfold. It will be removing a cancer from the German body politic which for generations has produced only misery and only pain to the whole world. . . .

A conference of all the United Nations of the world will meet in San Francisco on April 25, 1945. There, we all hope, and confidently expect, to execute a definite charter of organization under which the peace of the world will be preserved and the forces of aggression permanently outlawed.

This time we are not making the mistake of waiting until the end of the war to set up the machinery of peace. This time, as we fight together to win the war finally, we work together to keep it from happening again.

I – as you know – have always been a believer in the document called the Constitution of the United States. And I spent a good deal of time in educating two other Nations of the world in regard to the Constitution of the United States. The charter has to be – and should be – approved by the Senate of the United States, under the Constitution. I think the other Nations all know it now. I am aware of that fact, and now all the other Nations are. And we hope that the Senate will approve of what is set forth as the Charter of the United Nations when they all come together in San Francisco next month. . . .

The Senate and the House of Representatives will both be represented at the San Francisco Conference. The Congressional delegates to the San Francisco Conference will consist of an equal number of Republican and Democratic members. The American Delegation is – in every sense of the word – bipartisan.

World peace is not a party question. I think that Republicans want peace just as much as Democrats. It is not a party question – any more than is military victory – the winning of the war. . . .

The structure of world peace cannot be the work of one man, or one party, or one Nation. It cannot be just an American peace, or a British peace, or a Russian, a French, or a Chinese peace. It cannot be a peace of large Nations – or of small Nations. It must be a peace which rests on the cooperative effort of the whole world.

It cannot be a structure of complete perfection at first. But it can be a peace – and it will be a peace – based on the sound and just principles of the Atlantic Charter – on the concept of the dignity of the human being – and on the guarantees of tolerance and freedom of religious worship.

As the Allied armies have marched to military victory, they have liberated people whose liberties had been crushed by the Nazis for four long years, whose economy has been reduced to ruin by Nazi despoilers.

There have been instances of political confusion and unrest in these liberated areas – that is not unexpected – as in Greece or in Poland or in Yugoslavia, and there may be more. Worse than that, there actually began to grow up in some of these places queer ideas of, for instance, 'spheres of influence' that were incompatible with the basic principles of international collaboration. If allowed to go on unchecked, these developments might have had tragic results in time.

It is fruitless to try to place the blame for this situation on one particular Nation or on another. It is the kind of development that is almost inevitable unless the major powers of the world continue without interruption to work together and to assume joint responsibility for the solution of problems that may arise to endanger the peace of the world.

We met in the Crimea, determined to settle this matter of liberated areas. Things that might happen that we cannot foresee at this moment might happen suddenly – unexpectedly – next week or next month. And I am happy to confirm to the Congress that we did arrive at a settlement – and, incidentally, a unanimous settlement.

The three most powerful Nations have agreed that the political and economic problems of any area liberated from Nazi conquest, or of any former Axis satellite, are a joint responsibility of all three Governments. They will join together, during the temporary period of instability – after hostilities – to help the people of any liberated area, or of any former satellite state, to solve their own problems through firmly established democratic processes.

They will endeavor to see to it that the people who carry on the interim government between occupation of Germany and true independence, will be as representative as possible of all democratic elements in the population, and that free elections are held as soon as possible thereafter.

Responsibility for political conditions thousands of miles away can no longer be avoided by this great Nation. Certainly, I do not want to live to see another war. As I have said, the world is smaller – smaller every year. The United States now exerts a tremendous influence in the cause of peace throughout all the world. What we people over here are thinking and talking about is in the interest of peace, because it is known all over the world. The slightest remark in either House of the Congress is known all over the world the following day. We will continue to exert that influence, only if we are willing to continue to share in the responsibility for keeping the peace. It will be our own tragic loss, I think, if we were to shirk that responsibility.

The final decisions in these areas are going to be made jointly; and therefore they will often be a result of give-and-take compromise. The United States will not always have its way a hundred percent – nor will Russia nor Great Britain. We shall not always have ideal answers – solutions to complicated international problems, even though we are determined continuously to strive toward that ideal. But I am sure that under the agreements reached at Yalta, there will be a more stable political Europe than ever before.

Of course, once there has been a free expression of the people's will in any country, our immediate responsibility ends – with the exception only of such action as may be agreed on in the International Security Organization that we hope to set up. . . .

One outstanding example of joint action by the three major Allied powers in the liberated areas was the solution reached on Poland. The whole Polish question was a potential source of trouble in postwar Europe – as it has been sometimes before – and we came to the Conference determined to find a common ground for its solution. And we did – even though everybody does not agree with us, obviously.

Our objective was to help to create a strong, independent, and prosperous Nation. That is the thing we must always remember, those words, agreed to by Russia, by Britain, and by the United States: the objective of making Poland a strong, independent, and prosperous Nation, with a government ultimately to be selected by the Polish people themselves.

To achieve that objective, it was necessary to provide for the formation of a new government much more representative than had been possible while Poland was enslaved. There were, as you know, two governments – one in London, one in Lublin – practically in Russia. Accordingly, steps were taken at Yalta to reorganize the existing Provisional Government in Poland on a broader democratic basis, so as to include democratic leaders now in Poland and those abroad. This new, reorganized government will be recognized by all of us as the temporary government of Poland. Poland needs a temporary government in the worst way – an ad interim government, I think is another way of putting it.

However, the new Polish Provisional Government of National Unity will be pledged to holding a free election as soon as possible on the basis of universal suffrage and a secret ballot.

Throughout history, Poland has been the corridor through which attacks on Russia have been made. Twice in this generation, Germany has struck at Russia through this corridor. To insure European security and world peace, a strong and independent Poland is necessary to prevent that from happening again.

The decision with respect to the boundaries of Poland was, frankly, a compromise. I did not agree with all of it, by any means, but we did not go as far as Britain wanted, in certain areas; we did not go so far as Russia wanted, in certain areas; and we did not go so far as I wanted, in certain areas. It *was* a compromise. The decision is one, however, under which the Poles will receive compensation in territory in the North and West in exchange for what they lose by the Curzon Line in the East. The limits of the western border will be permanently fixed in the final Peace Conference. We know, roughly, that it will include – in the new, strong Poland – quite a large slice of what now is called Germany. And it was agreed, also, that the new Poland will have a large and long coast line, and many new harbors. Also, that most of East Prussia will go to Poland. A corner of it will go to Russia. Also, that the anomaly of the Free State of Danzig will come to an end; I think Danzig would be a lot better if it were Polish.

It is well known that the people east of the Curzon Line – just for example, here is why I compromised – are predominantly white Russian and Ukrainian – they are not Polish; and a very great majority of the people west of the line are predominantly Polish, except in that part of East Prussia and eastern Germany, which will go to the new Poland. As far back as 1919, representatives of the Allies agreed that the Curzon Line represented a fair boundary between the two peoples. And you must remember, also, that there had not been any Polish government before 1919 for a great many generations.

I am convinced that the agreement on Poland, under the circumstances, is the most hopeful agreement possible for a free, independent, and prosperous Polish state. . . .

The Conference in the Crimea was a turning point – I hope in our history and therefore in the history of the world. There will soon be presented to the Senate of the United States and to the American people a great decision that will determine the fate of the United States – and of the world – for generations to come.

There can be no middle ground here. We shall have to take the responsibility for world collaboration, or we shall have to bear the responsibility for another world conflict.

I know that the word 'planning' is not looked upon with favor in some circles. In domestic affairs, tragic mistakes have been made by reason of lack of planning; and, on the other hand, many great improvements in living, and many benefits to the human race, have been accomplished as a result of adequate, intelligent planning – reclamation of desert areas, developments of whole river valleys, and provision for adequate housing.

The same will be true in relations between Nations. For the second time in the lives of most of us this generation is face to face with the objective of preventing wars. To meet that objective, the Nations of the world will either have a plan or they will not. The groundwork of a plan has now been furnished, and has been submitted to humanity for discussion and decision.

No plan is perfect. Whatever is adopted at San Francisco will doubtless have to be amended time and again over the years, just as our own Constitution has been.

No one can say exactly how long any plan will last. Peace can endure only so long as humanity really insists upon it, and is willing to work for it – and sacrifice for it.

Twenty-five years ago, American fighting men looked to the statesmen of the world to finish the work of peace for which they fought and suffered. We failed them then. We cannot fail them again, and expect the world again to survive.

The Crimea Conference was a successful effort by the three leading Nations to find a common ground for peace. It ought to spell the end of the system of unilateral action, the exclusive alliances, the spheres of influence, the balances of power, and all the other expedients that have been tried for centuries – and have always failed.

We propose to substitute for all these, a universal organization in which all peace-loving Nations will finally have a chance to join.

I am confident that the Congress and the American people will accept the results of this Conference as the beginnings of a permanent structure of peace upon which we can begin to build, under God, that better world in which our children and grandchildren – yours and mine, the children and grandchildren of the whole world – must live, and can live.

And that, my friends, is the principal message I can give you. But I feel it very deeply, as I know that all of you are feeling it today, and are going to feel it in the future.

The Public Papers and Addresses of Franklin D. Roosevelt (New York, 1950), Vol. 13, pp. 570–586 (excerpts)

(b) *Excerpts from the last correspondence between Roosevelt, Stalin, and Churchill*

President Roosevelt to Marshal Stalin *4 Apr. 45*

I have received with astonishment your message of April 3 containing an allegation that arrangements which were made between Field-Marshal Alexander and Kesselring at Berne 'permitted the Anglo-American troops to advance to the east, and the Anglo-Americans promised in return to ease for the Germans the peace terms.'

In my previous messages to you in regard to the attempts made in Berne to arrange a conference to discuss a surrender of the German Army in Italy I have told you that (i) no negotiations were held in Berne; (ii) that the meeting had no political implications whatever; (iii) that in any surrender of the enemy Army in Italy there could be no violation of our agreed principle of unconditional surrender; (iv) that Soviet officers would be welcomed at any meeting that might be arranged to discuss surrender.

For the advantage of our common war effort against Germany,

which today gives excellent promise of an early success in a disintegration of the German armies, I must continue to assume that you have the same high confidence in my truthfulness and reliability that I have always had in yours.

I have also a full appreciation of the effect your gallant Army has had in making possible a crossing of the Rhine by the forces under General Eisenhower, and the effect that your forces will have hereafter on the eventual collapse of the German resistance to our combined attacks.

I have complete confidence in General Eisenhower, and know that he certainly would inform me before entering into any agreement with the Germans. He is instructed to demand, and will demand, unconditional surrender of enemy troops that may be defeated on his front. Our advances on the Western Front are due to military action. Their speed has been attributable mainly to the terrific impact of our air-power, resulting in destruction of German communications, and to the fact that Eisenhower was able to cripple the bulk of the German forces on the Western Front while they were still west of the Rhine.

I am certain that there were no negotiations in Berne at any time, and I feel that your information to that effect must have come from German sources, which have made persistent efforts to create dissension between us in order to escape in some measure responsibility for their war crimes. If that was Wolff's purpose in Berne your message proves that he has had some success.

With a confidence in your belief in my personal reliability and in my determination to bring about together with you an unconditional surrender of the Nazis, it is astonishing that a belief seems to have reached the Soviet Government that I have entered into an agreement with the enemy without first obtaining your full agreement.

Finally I would say this: it would be one of the great tragedies of history if at the very moment of the victory now within our grasp such distrust, such lack of faith, should prejudice the entire undertaking after the colossal losses of life, material and treasure involved.

Frankly, I cannot avoid a feeling of bitter resentment toward your informers, whoever they are, for such vile misrepresentations of my actions or those of my trusted subordinates.

President Roosevelt to Marshal Stalin *12 Apr. 45*

Thank you for your frank explanation of the Soviet point of view of the Berne incident, which now appears to have faded into the past without having accomplished any useful purpose.

There must not, in any event, be mutual distrust, and minor misunderstandings of this character should not arise in the future. I feel sure that when our armies make contact in Germany and join in a fully co-ordinated offensive the Nazis' armies will disintegrate.

President Roosevelt to Prime Minister *12 Apr. 45*

I would minimise the general Soviet problem as much as possible, because these problems, in one form or another, seem to arise every day, and most of them straighten out, as in the case of the Berne meeting.

We must be firm, however, and our course thus far is correct.

Papers Relating to the Foreign Relations of the United States, 1945 (Washington, 1967), Vol. III, pp. 745-6 and p. 756; Vol. V, p. 210

7 The Opening of the Atomic Age

(a) *Statement by President Harry S. Truman on the Bombing of Hiroshima, August 6, 1945*

Sixteen hours ago an American airplane dropped one bomb on Hiroshima, an important Japanese Army base. That bomb had more power than 20,000 tons of TNT. It had more than two thousand times the blast power of the British 'Grand Slam' which is the largest bomb ever yet used in the history of warfare.

The Japanese began the war from the air at Pearl Harbor. They have been repaid manyfold. And the end is not yet. With this bomb we have now added a new and revolutionary increase in destruction to supplement the growing power of our armed forces. In their present form these bombs are now in production and even more powerful forms are in development.

It is an atomic bomb. It is a harnessing of the basic power of the universe. The force from which the sun draws its powers has been loosed against those who brought war to the Far East. . . .

We are now prepared to obliterate more rapidly and completely every productive enterprise the Japanese have above ground in any city. We shall destroy their docks, their factories and their communications. Let there be no mistake; we shall completely destroy Japan's power to make war.

It was to spare the Japanese people from utter destruction that the ultimatum of July 26 was issued at Potsdam. Their leaders promptly rejected that ultimatum. If they do not now accept our terms they may expect a rain of ruin from the air, the like of which has never been seen on this earth. Behind this air attack will follow sea and land forces in such numbers and power as they have not yet seen and with the fighting skill of which they are already well aware. . . .

The fact that we can release atomic energy ushers in a new era in man's understanding of nature's forces. Atomic energy may, in the future, supplement the power that now comes from coal, oil and falling water, but at present it cannot be produced on a basis to compete with them commercially. Before that comes there must be a long period of intensive research.

It has never been the habit of the scientists of this country or the policy of this Government to withhold from the world scientific knowledge. Normally, therefore, everything about this work with atomic energy would be made public.

But under present circumstances it is not intended to divulge the terminal processes of production or all the military applications, pending further examination of possible methods of protecting us and the rest of the world from the danger of sudden destruction.

I shall recommend that the Congress of the United States consider promptly the establishment of an appropriate commission to control the production and use of atomic power within the United States. I shall give further consideration and make further recommendations to the Congress as to how atomic power can become a powerful and forceful influence toward the maintenance of world peace.

Documents on American Foreign Relations, 1945, (Princeton, N.J., 1947), Vol. VII, pp. 419–21 (excerpts)

(b) *Secretary Henry L. Stimson's Memorandum to President Truman on Control of Atomic Weapons, September 11, 1945*

MEMORANDUM FOR THE PRESIDENT

11 September 1945

Subject: Proposed Action for Control of Atomic Bombs.

The advent of the atomic bomb has stimulated great military and probably even greater political interest throughout the civilized world. In a world atmosphere already extremely sensitive to power, the introduction of this weapon has profoundly affected political considerations in all sections of the globe.

In many quarters it has been interpreted as a substantial offset to the growth of Russian influence on the continent. We can be certain that the Soviet Government has sensed this tendency and the temptation will be strong for the Soviet political and military leaders to acquire this weapon in the shortest possible time. Britain in effect already has the status of a partner with us in the development of this weapon. Accordingly, unless the Soviets are voluntarily invited into the partnership upon a basis of co-operation and trust, we are going to maintain the Anglo-Saxon bloc over against the Soviet in the possession of this weapon. Such a condition will almost certainly stimulate feverish activity on the part of the Soviet towards the development of this bomb in what will in effect be a secret armament race of a rather desperate character. There is evidence to indicate that such activity may have already commenced.

If we feel, as I assume we must, that civilization demands that someday we shall arrive at a satisfactory international arrangement respecting the control of this new force, the question then is how long we can afford to enjoy our momentary superiority in the hope of achieving our immediate peace council objectives.

Whether Russia gets control of the necessary secrets of production in a minimum of say four years or a maximum of twenty years is not nearly as important to the world and civilization as to make sure that when they do get it they are willing and co-operative partners among the peace-loving nations of the world. It is true if we approach them now, as I would propose, we may be gambling on their good faith and risk their getting into production of bombs a little sooner than they would otherwise.

To put the matter concisely, I consider the problem of our satisfactory relations with Russia as not merely connected with but as virtually dominated by the problem of the atomic bomb. Except for the problem of the control of that bomb, those relations, while vitally important, might not be immediately pressing. The establishment of relations of mutual confidence between her and us could afford to await the slow progress of time. But with the discovery of the bomb, they became immediately emergent. *Those relations may be perhaps irretrievably embittered by the way in which we approach the solution of the bomb with Russia. For if we fail to approach them now and merely continue to negotiate with them, having this weapon rather ostentatiously on our hip, their suspicions and their distrust of our purposes and motives will increase.* It will inspire them to greater efforts in an all-out effort to solve the problem. If the solution is achieved in that spirit, it is much less likely that we will ever get the kind of covenant we may desperately need in the future. This risk is, I believe, greater than the other, inasmuch as our objective must be to get the best kind of international bargain we can – one that has some chance of being kept and saving civilization not for five or for twenty years, but forever.

The chief lesson I have learned in a long life is that the only way you can make a man trustworthy is to trust him; and the surest way to make him untrustworthy is to distrust him and show your distrust.

If the atomic bomb were merely another though more devastating military weapon to be assimilated into our pattern of international relations, it would be one thing. We could then follow the old custom of secrecy and nationalistic military superiority relying on international caution to prescribe the future use of the weapon as we did with gas. But I think the bomb instead constitutes merely a first step in a new control by man over the forces of nature too revolutionary and dangerous to fit into the old concepts. I think it really caps the climax of the race between man's growing technical power for destructiveness and his psychological power of self-control and group control – his moral power. If so, our method of approach to the Russians is a question of the most vital importance in the evolution of human progress.

Since the crux of the problem is Russia, any contemplated action leading to the control of this weapon should be primarily directed *to* Russia. It is my judgment that the Soviet would be more apt to respond sincerely to a direct and forthright approach made by the United States on this subject than would be the case if the approach were made as a part of a general international scheme, or if the approach were made after a succession of express or implied threats or near threats in our peace negotiations.

My idea of an approach to the Soviets would be a direct proposal after discussion with the British that we would be prepared in effect to enter an arrangement with the Russians, the general purpose of which would be to control and limit the use of the atomic bomb as an instrument of war and so far as possible to direct and encourage the development of atomic power for peaceful and humanitarian purposes. Such an approach might more specifically lead to the proposal that we would stop work on the further improvement in, or manufacture of, the bomb as a military weapon, provided the Russians and the British would agree to do likewise. It might also provide that we would be willing to impound what bombs we now have in the United States provided the Russians and the British would agree with us that in no event will they or we use a bomb as an instrument of war unless all three Governments agree to that use. We might also consider including in the arrangement a covenant with the U.K. and the Soviets providing for the exchange of benefits of future developments whereby atomic energy may be applied on a mutually satisfactory basis for commercial or humanitarian purposes.

I would make such an approach just as soon as our immediate political considerations make it appropriate.

I emphasize perhaps beyond all other considerations the importance of taking this action with Russia as a proposal of the United States – backed by Great Britain but peculiarly the proposal of the United States. Action of any international group of nations, including many small nations who have not demonstrated their potential power or responsibility in this war would not, in my opinion, be taken seriously by the Soviets. The loose debates which would surround such proposal, if put before a conference of nations, would provoke but scant favor from the Soviet. As I say, I think this is the most important point in the program. . . .

Papers Relating to the Foreign Relations of the United States, 1945 Vol. II (Washington, 1967), pp. 41–4

VI

THE COLD WAR AND THE REVOLUTION IN AMERICAN FOREIGN POLICY

Historians now vigorously debate the origins of and responsibilities for the Cold War. Did it begin in the spring of 1945? Or did it start back in 1917 when Bolshevism was born? Was the United States the idealistic innocent duped by Russian promises or did capitalist America, as the New Left suggests, initiate the Cold War by brandishing its bomb to thwart the legitimate security needs of the Soviet Union? The controversies will long rage and no set of documents can fully answer questions which ultimately depend upon individual interpretation. Nevertheless, selected documents can suggest guidelines and point to major stages in the evolution of the East-West conflict that began even before the last guns of World War II had fallen silent.

One of the first Americans to express strong suspicion of the Russians was James Forrestal, then Truman's Secretary of the Navy and soon to become his first Secretary of Defence when the three military services were unified. His diary faithfully records the growing hostility that more than a few Americans were beginning to feel in 1945 and 1946 (1). But even more important were the actions taken by the United States as the Cold War began to intensify. For the first time in its history the United States began a systematic effort to co-ordinate the heretofore separate strands of military and diplomatic policy into what it was hoped would be a unified national security policy. The creation of the National Security Council, an institution that on many subsequent occasions proved more significant than the cabinet, was a major climax in post-war administrative reorganisation. Again it is the Forrestal diary that best indicates the role that the National Security Council was intended to fulfill (**2** (**a**), **2** (**b**)).

But the real revolution began in 1947 when, after two years of uncertainty and hesitation, the United States began to hammer out the policies – subsumed under the general heading of 'containment' – which laid the foundation for post-war diplomacy. The first of these, the Truman Doctrine, was hastily assembled in an atmosphere of crisis in the spring of 1947 when the British apparently without warning, notified Washington that they could no longer continue to support Greece and Turkey. The Truman Doctrine bears every sign of being a committee document, a creation of scissors and paste, and many of its implications – for example, the sweeping promise of assistance to all 'free peoples' – had not been thought through (3 (**a**)).

The major American effort was the Marshall Plan, named for Secretary of State George Marshall who first outlined the basic concepts in a speech at graduation ceremonies at Harvard University in June 1947. The Marshall Plan was a vast economic endeavour designed to combat Communism by rebuilding the shattered economies of Europe, and its authors clearly hoped to offer something more concrete and positive than the somewhat sterile anti-communism of the Truman Doctrine (3 (**b**)).

With the Berlin blockade and the *coup* in Czechoslovakia containment moved from its economic to its military phase. The Truman administration now clearly believed that the Soviet threat was no longer internal, to be met by economic measures, but external and military. With the signing of the North Atlantic Treaty in 1949 the United States completed the revolution in its military and foreign policies that had begun two years earlier. America, the great neutral of 1914, the ambivalent bystander of 1939, had become not merely a partner in but the prime mover of a system of peacetime military alliances (3 (**c**)).

But, as in 1940–41 there was bitter, often divisive debate. There was a modest onslaught from the political Left; Henry Wallace, once Roosevelt's Vice-President, verbalised the fears of those who thought that America was becoming militarised, neglecting the United Nations, and falling victim to hysterical anti-communism (4 (**a**)). But the Wallace movement struck little political fire, and in the 1948 election Wallace polled but a fragment of the total vote. Arguments from the Left similar to those first raised by Wallace did not reappear as a significant criticism of American foreign policy until the 1960s. Far more important was the attack from the Right, an attack symbolised by the reckless excesses of the junior senator from Wisconsin, Joe McCarthy. In speech after speech McCarthy charged that the Truman administration was infiltrated by Communists and that loyal Americans had been victimised by 'twenty years of treason'. The noxious effects of McCarthyism can scarcely be exaggerated: it fostered a mindless, militant anti-communism which, in turn, created grave doubts throughout the world about the stability of American democracy and, at home, so restricted the options of the Democratic administration that President Truman became literally the prisoner of his right-wing critics (4 (**b**)).

McCarthyism fed upon many American frustrations: apparent Communist successes throughout the world, the revelation that the Soviet Union had developed atomic weapons and the trial and conviction of Alger Hiss, one time State Department official charged with Communist affiliations. But above all it evolved out of the national mood created by the collapse of Nationalist China. Americans simply could not accept the fact that Chiang kai-shek had been driven from the mainland by his Communist rivals. Far too many Americans accepted the simplistic answer that the Truman administration had 'sold China down the river' or, worse, agreed with Joe McCarthy that the only possible explanation was treason in the Department of State. Secretary Acheson, in a vain effort to tame the whirlwind, prepared a detailed 'White Paper' on Chinese-American relations. His letter of transmittal forcefully stated the Administration's position, but the 'White Paper' failed to convince the critics and the debate raged on (5).

In June of 1950 the Korean war erupted and the United States went to the military assistance of South Korea. When the Chinese Communists intervened in November, debate over Far Eastern policy became completely out of control. And the Korean War became (until Vietnam) the most unpopular war in all American history. The Truman administration sought to wage a limited war for limited objectives. It feared that expansion of the conflict might trigger off World War III; it believed that the principal Communist objectives still lay in Europe rather than Asia; and it heeded the wishes of its European allies who opposed any expansion of the conflict. All of these assumptions were challenged by the Republican party and, above all, by the Supreme Commander in the Far East, General Douglas MacArthur. MacArthur and his supporters were bitter about the checks which alliance policy imposed upon the United States and argued that America should 'go it alone if necessary'. They believed that the only proper objective in war is victory and they were convinced that Asia was more vital than Europe. When Truman relieved MacArthur in the spring of 1951, the resulting dissension had no parallel in American history. MacArthur pleaded his case in a dramatic, emotional speech before both houses of Congress (**6 (a)**). The Administration's arguments for limited war were best presented by General Omar Bradley when he testified before a special Congressional committee (**6 (b)**).

Although the furor created by the dismissal of MacArthur eventually quietened down, none of the fundamental issues of Far Eastern policy were solved as long as Truman remained in the White House. The great debates over foreign policy continued. In the spring of 1952, as the Presidential campaign began to shape up, John Foster Dulles gave vent to the prevailing Republican criticism of the Truman policies in an article published in *Life* magazine. His call for boldness in foreign policy was both a critique of containment as well as a remarkable forecast of the policies (massive retaliation, the 'New Look' in military posture) and some of the will-o'-the-wisps (liberation, regaining the initiative) that he would pursue as Dwight Eisenhower's Secretary of State after January of 1953 (7).

Although this volume ends with the Truman years, a short postscript is required. The Eisenhower administration secured a truce in Korea and accepted, however reluctantly, the Geneva Accords on Vietnam. Indeed, for all the verbiage and rhetoric in the *Life* article, Dulles actually continued the containment policy far more than he innovated. In point of fact Eisenhower and Dulles actually carried through and consolidated the policies of the diplomatic and military revolution they had inherited from their Democratic predecessors.

I The Origins of the Cold War

Excerpts from the Diaries of James Forrestal, April 20, 1945 and August 15, 1946

20 April 1945 *Russia*

I saw Averell Harriman, the American Ambassador to Russia, last night. He stated his strong apprehensions as to the future of our relations with Russia unless our entire attitude toward them became characterized by much greater firmness. He said that, using the fear of Germany as a stalking horse, they would continue on their program of setting up states around their borders which would follow the same idology as the Russians. He said the outward thrust of Communism was not dead and that we might well have to face an ideological warfare just as vigorous and dangerous as Fascism or Nazism.

15 August 1946 *Meeting with President*

Meeting with the President at 3:30. Dean Acheson stated the background of U.S.S.R.'s note of this week to Turkey. . . . The Under Secretary of State said that the War, State and Navy Departments had canvassed the situation thoroughly – that it was the view of the State Department that the Russian note and its last three demands on Turkey reflected a desire to control and dominate that country; that acceding to these demands would be followed next by infiltration and domination of Greece by Russia with the obvious consequences in the Middle East and the obvious threat to the line of communications of the British to India. He said that he felt that this trial balloon of the Russians should be firmly resented by the President with the full realization that if Russia did not back down and if we maintained our attitude it might lead to armed conflict. The President replied that he was perfectly clear we should take a firm position both in this instance and in China; that we might as well find out whether the Russians were bent on world conquest now as in five or ten years.

The Under Secretary of War recommended that in view of the seriousness which the State Department attached to the position we planned to take, steps should be undertaken to inform the country of the background of the decision, particularly of the implications contained in the Russian note. I added further that we should set in motion machinery to see to it that people on the [*New York*] *Times* and [*New York Herald*] *Tribune* and other newspapers should be briefed on the factual background.

Walter Millis, ed., *The Forrestal Diaries* (New York, 1951), pp. 47, 192. Printed by permission of the WCC Publishing Co.

2 The Coordination of Military and Foreign Policy

(a) *Creation of the National Security Council: Excerpts from the report of Ferdinand Eberstadt, September 25, 1945*

SUMMARY OF CONCLUSIONS

> . . . *What changes in the present relationships of the military services and departments has our war experience indicated as desirable to improve our national security?*

Experience in the late war has revealed serious weaknesses in our present organizational set-up – weaknesses between and within the services, as well as in their relationships to other important elements concerned with our national security.

Mostly they were defects of coordination. Gaps between foreign and military policy – between the State Department and the Military Establishments. Gaps between strategic planning and its logistic implementation – between the Joint Chiefs of Staff and the military and civilian agencies responsible for industrial mobilization. Gaps between and within the military services – principally in the field of procurement and logistics. Gaps in information and intelligence – between the executive and legislative branches of our Government, between the several departments, and between Government and the people.

We have concluded that these faults were due principally to lack of appropriate and seasoned mechanisms and of adequate plans, policies, and procedures for coordination; lack of clear understanding and appreciation by one group or individual of the relation of others to the over-all job. These ills are susceptible of cure without dangerous experiments with our present set-up. . . .

We thus come to your final question.

> *What form of postwar organization should be established and maintained to enable the military services and other Government departments and agencies most effectively to provide for and protect our national security?*

The question of the form of organization of our military forces must be viewed in its proper perspective as only one part of a much larger picture encompassing many elements, military and civilian, governmental and private, which contribute to our national security and defense. It is obviously impossible to unify all these elements under one command, short of the President. . . .

The necessity of integrating all these elements into an alert, smoothly working, and efficient machine is more important now than ever before. Such integration is compelled by our present world commitments and risks, by the tremendously increased scope and tempo of modern warfare, and by the epochal scientific discoveries culminating in the atomic bomb.

This will involve, among others, organizational ties between the Department of State and the military departments, ties between the military departments in strategy and logistics, ties between the military departments and the agencies responsible for planning and carrying out mobilization of our industrial and human resources, between the gathering of information and intelligence and its dissemination and use, between scientific advances and their military application.

The next war will probably break out with little or no warning and will almost immediately achieve its maximum tempo of violence and destruction. Contrasting with the shortened opportunity for defensive preparation is the increased length of time necessary to prepare the complicated offensive and defensive weapons and organizational structure essential to modern warfare.

The nation not fully prepared will be at a greater disadvantage than ever before.

The great need, therefore, is that we be prepared always and all along the line, not simply to defend ourselves after an attack, but through all available political, military, and economic means to forestall any such attack. The knowledge that we are so prepared and alert will in itself be a great influence for world peace.

Much has been said about the importance of waging peace, as well as war. We have tried to suggest an organizational structure adapted to both purposes. . . .

Creation of a National Security Council

To afford a permanent vehicle for maintaining active, close, and continuous contact between the departments and agencies of our Government responsible, respectively, for our foreign and military policies and their implementation, we recommend the establishment of a National Security Council.

The National Security Council would be the keystone of our organizational structure for national security.

It should be charged with the duty (1) of formulating and coordinating over-all policies in the political and military fields, (2) of assessing and appraising our foreign objectives, commitments and risks, and (3) of keeping these in balance with our military power, in being and potential.

It would be a policy-forming and advisory, not an executive, body.

Its membership should consist of the Secretaries of State, War, Navy, and Air, and the Chairman of the National Security Resources Board. . . . Provision should be made for such additions to its membership as the President may from time to time deem proper.

Unification of the War and Navy Departments and Post-war Organization for National Security. Report of Ferdinand Eberstadt to Secretary of the Navy James Forrestal (Washington, 1945) (79th Congress, 1st Session, Senate Committee Report, October 23, 1945)

(b) *The Role of the National Security Council: excerpt from the Forrestal Diaries, September 22, 1947*

22 September 1947 *Meeting with War and Security Councils*

Meeting in my office today, following present: Royall, Symington and Sullivan, Eisenhower, Nimitz, Spaatz, Souers, Gruenther and Leva.

I said the purpose of the meeting was a preliminary discussion of procedures in the War Council [composed of the four Defense Secretaries and the three Chiefs of Staff] and in the Security Council, what category of subjects the War Council should discuss and in what form they should be transmitted to the Security Council. The question arose as to whether the Security Council should make positive recommendations as to matters of policy and to whom they should make them. Secretary Royall stated that the council *should* make such recommendations. I expressed the view that we would have to be most careful to avoid (a) the appearance of either duplicating or replacing the functions of the Cabinet, and (b) giving the public the impression that our foreign policy was completely dominated by a military point of view.

I reported a conversation I had this morning with [Under] Secretary

Lovett of the State Department on the question of Italy – whether if upon evacuation by American troops there should be subsequent formation of a Communist republic in the north, we should encourage an invitation from De Gasperi's government to send a military mission to Italy to reconstitute their army and otherwise put them in a position to resist Communist domination. I said that Lovett had made the statement that neither he nor the State Department was in a position to evaluate our capabilities in this direction. I had responded, I said, that by the same token the military Services were in no position to determine national policy on such a matter; that it was our job only to state the capabilities and then await instructions. Lovett said because of this mixture of interest between our two sides of government, it was obvious to him that such a subject afforded an example of what kind of business should come before the Security Council. I agreed and set some time during Friday for such a meeting.

Other subjects discussed briefly were Korea, the United Nations Police Force, and the work of the Committee on the Reduction of Conventional Armaments.

Forrestal Diaries, pp. 317–18

3 The Revolution in American Foreign Policy

(a) *The Truman Doctrine: Message of President Harry Truman to the Congress on Greek–Turkish Aid, March 12, 1947*

MR. PRESIDENT, MR. SPEAKER, MEMBERS OF THE CONGRESS OF THE UNITED STATES:

The gravity of the situation which confronts the world today necessitates my appearance before a joint session of the Congress.

The foreign policy and the national security of this country are involved.

One aspect of the present situation, which I wish to present to you at this time for your consideration and decision, concerns Greece and Turkey.

The United States has received from the Greek Government an urgent appeal for financial and economic assistance. Preliminary reports from the American Economic Mission now in Greece and reports from the American Ambassador in Greece corroborate the statement of the Greek Government that assistance is imperative if Greece is to survive as a free nation.

I do not believe that the American people and the Congress wish to turn a deaf ear to the appeal of the Greek Government.

Greece is not a rich country. Lack of sufficient natural resources has always forced the Greek people to work hard to make both ends meet. Since 1940 this industrious and peace-loving country has suffered invasion, four years of cruel enemy occupation, and bitter internal strife. . . .

As a result of these tragic conditions, a militant minority, exploiting human want and misery, was able to create political chaos which, until now, has made economic recovery impossible.

Greece is today without funds to finance the importation of those goods which are essential to bare subsistence. Under these circumstances the people of Greece cannot make progress in solving their problems of reconstruction. Greece is in desperate need of financial and economic assistance to enable it to resume purchases of food, clothing, fuel, and seeds. These are indispensable for the subsistence of its people and are obtainable only from abroad. Greece must have help to import the goods necessary to restore internal order and security so essential for economic and political recovery. . . .

The very existence of the Greek state is today threatened by the terrorist activities of several thousand armed men, led by Communists, who defy the Government's authority at a number of points, particularly along the northern boundaries. A commission appointed by the United Nations Security Council is at present investigating disturbed conditions in northern Greece and alleged border violations along the frontier between Greece on the one hand and Albania, Bulgaria, and Yugoslavia on the other. . . .

Greece must have assistance if it is to become a self-supporting and self-respecting democracy.

The United States must supply that assistance. We have already extended to Greece certain types of relief and economic aid, but these are inadequate.

There is no other country to which democratic Greece can turn.

No other nation is willing and able to provide the necessary support for a democratic Greek Government.

The British Government, which has been helping Greece, can give no further financial or economic aid after March 31. Great Britain finds itself under the necessity of reducing or liquidating its commitments in several parts of the world, including Greece.

We have considered how the United Nations might assist in this crisis. But the situation is an urgent one requiring immediate action and the United Nations and its related organizations are not in a position to extend help of the kind that is required. . . .

The Greek Government has been operating in an atmosphere of chaos and extremism. It has made mistakes. The extension of aid by this country does not mean that the United States condones everything that the Greek Government has done or will do. We have condemned in the past, and we condemn now, extremist measures of the right or the left. We have in the past advised tolerance, and we advise tolerance now.

Greece's neighbor, Turkey, also deserves our attention.

The future of Turkey as an independent and economically sound state is clearly no less important to the freedom-loving peoples of the world than the future of Greece. The circumstances in which Turkey finds itself today are considerably different from those of Greece. Turkey has been spared the disasters that have beset Greece. And during the war the United States and Great Britain furnished Turkey with material aid.

Nevertheless, Turkey now needs our support.

Since the war Turkey has sought additional financial assistance from Great Britain and the United States for the purpose of effecting that modernization necessary for the maintenance of its national integrity.

That integrity is essential to the preservation of order in the Middle East.

The British Government has informed us that, owing to its own difficulties, it can no longer extend financial or economic aid to Turkey.

As in the case of Greece, if Turkey is to have the assistance it needs, the United States must supply it. We are the only country able to provide that help.

I am fully aware of the broad implications involved if the United States extends assistance to Greece and Turkey, and I shall discuss these implications with you at this time.

One of the primary objectives of the foreign policy of the United States is the creation of conditions in which we and other nations will be able to work out a way of life free from coercion. This was a fundamental issue in the war with Germany and Japan. Our victory was won over countries which sought to impose their will, and their way of life, upon other nations.

To insure the peaceful development of nations, free from coercion, the United States has taken a leading part in establishing the United

Nations. The United Nations is designed to make possible lasting freedom and independence for all its members. We shall not realize our objectives, however, unless we are willing to help free peoples to maintain their free institutions and their national integrity against aggressive movements that seek to impose upon them totalitarian regimes. This is no more than a frank recognition that totalitarian regimes imposed upon free peoples, by direct or indirect aggression, undermine the foundations of international peace and hence the security of the United States.

At the present moment in world history nearly every nation must choose between alternative ways of life. The choice is too often not a free one.

One way of life is based upon the will of the majority, and is distinguished by free institutions, representative government, free elections, guarantees of individual liberty, freedom of speech and religion, and freedom from political oppression.

The second way of life is based upon the will of a minority forcibly imposed upon the majority. It relies upon terror and oppression, a controlled press and radio, fixed elections, and the suppression of personal freedoms.

I believe that it must be the policy of the United States to support free peoples who are resisting attempted subjugation by armed minorities or by outside pressures.

I believe that we must assist free peoples to work out their own destinies in their own way.

I believe that our help should be primarily through economic and financial aid which is essential to economic stability and orderly political processes.

The world is not static, and the *status quo* is not sacred. But we cannot allow changes in the *status quo* in violation of the Charter of the United Nations by such methods as coercion, or by such subterfuges as political infiltration. In helping free and independent nations to maintain their freedom, the United States will be giving effect to the principles of the Charter of the United Nations.

It is necessary only to glance at a map to realize that the survival and integrity of the Greek nation are of grave importance in a much wider situation. If Greece should fall under the control of an armed minority, the effect upon its neighbor, Turkey, would be immediate and serious. Confusion and disorder might well spread throughout the entire Middle East. . . .

I therefore ask the Congress to provide authority for assistance to

Greece and Turkey in the amount of $400,000,000 for the period ending June 30, 1948. In requesting these funds, I have taken into consideration the maximum amount of relief assistance which would be furnished to Greece out of the $350,000,000 which I recently requested that the Congress authorize for the prevention of starvation and suffering in countries devastated by the war.

In addition to funds, I ask the Congress to authorize the detail of American civilian and military personnel to Greece and Turkey, at the request of those countries, to assist in the tasks of reconstruction, and for the purpose of supervising the use of such financial and material assistance as may be furnished. I recommend that authority also be provided for the instruction and training of selected Greek and Turkish personnel. . . .

The seeds of totalitarian regimes are nurtured by misery and want. They spread and grow in the evil soil of poverty and strife. They reach their full growth when the hope of a people for a better life has died.

We must keep that hope alive.

The free peoples of the world look to us for support in maintaining their freedoms.

If we falter in our leadership, we may endanger the peace of the world – and we shall surely endanger the welfare of our own Nation.

Great responsibilities have been placed upon us by the swift movement of events.

I am confident that the Congress will face these responsibilities squarely.

A Decade of American Foreign Policy, 1941–1949,
pp. 1253-7 (excerpts)

(b) *The Marshall Plan: Address of Secretary of State George C. Marshall at Harvard University, June 5, 1947*

I need not tell you gentlemen that the world situation is very serious. That must be apparent to all intelligent people. I think one difficulty is that the problem is one of such enormous complexity that the very mass of facts presented to the public by press and radio make it exceedingly difficult for the man in the street to reach a clear appraisement of the situation. Furthermore, the people of this country are distant from the troubled areas of the earth and it is hard for them to comprehend the plight and consequent reactions of the long-suffering peoples, and the effect of those reactions on their governments in connection with our efforts to promote peace in the world.

In considering the requirements for the rehabilitation of Europe, the physical loss of life, the visible destruction of cities, factories, mines, and railroads was correctly estimated, but it has become obvious during recent months that this visible destruction was probably less serious than the dislocation of the entire fabric of European economy. For the past 10 years conditions have been highly abnormal. The feverish preparation for war and the more feverish maintenance of the war effort engulfed all aspects of national economies. Machinery has fallen into disrepair or is entirely obsolete. Under the arbitrary and destructive Nazi rule, virtually every possible enterprise was geared into the German war machine. Long-standing commercial ties, private institutions, banks, insurance companies, and shipping companies disappeared, through loss of capital, absorption through nationalization, or by simple destruction. In many countries, confidence in the local currency has been severely shaken. The breakdown of the business structure of Europe during the war was complete. Recovery has been seriously retarded by the fact that two years after the close of hostilities a peace settlement with Germany and Austria has not been agreed upon. But even given a more prompt solution of these difficult problems, the rehabilitation of the economic structure of Europe quite evidently will require a much longer time and greater effort than had been foreseen.

There is a phase of this matter which is both interesting and serious. The farmer has always produced the foodstuffs to exchange with the city dweller for the other necessities of life. This division of labor is the basis of modern civilization. At the present time it is threatened with breakdown. The town and city industries are not producing adequate goods to exchange with the food-producing farmer. Raw materials and fuel are in short supply. Machinery is lacking or worn out. The farmer or the peasant cannot find the goods for sale which he desires to purchase. So the sale of his farm produce for money which he cannot use seems to him an unprofitable transaction. He, therefore, has withdrawn many fields from crop cultivation and is using them for grazing. He feeds more grain to stock and finds for himself and his family an ample supply of food, however short he may be on clothing and the other ordinary gadgets of civilization. Meanwhile people in the cities are short of food and fuel. So the governments are forced to use their foreign money and credits to procure these necessities abroad. This process exhausts funds which are urgently needed for reconstruction. Thus a very serious situation is rapidly developing which bodes no good for the world. The modern system of the division of labor upon which the exchange of products is based is in danger of breaking down.

The truth of the matter is that Europe's requirements for the next three or four years of foreign food and other essential products – principally from America – are so much greater than her present ability to pay that she must have substantial additional help or face economic, social, and political deterioration of a very grave character.

The remedy lies in breaking the vicious circle and restoring the confidence of the European people in the economic future of their own countries and of Europe as a whole. The manufacturer and the farmer throughout wide areas must be able and willing to exchange their products for currencies the continuing value of which is not open to question.

Aside from the demoralizing effect on the world at large and the possibilities of disturbances arising as a result of the desperation of the people concerned, the consequences to the economy of the United States should be apparent to all. It is logical that the United States should do whatever it is able to do to assist in the return of normal economic health in the world, without which there can be no political stability and no assured peace. Our policy is directed not against any country or doctrine but against hunger, poverty, desperation, and chaos. Its purpose should be the revival of a working economy in the world so as to permit the emergence of political and social conditions in which free institutions can exist. Such assistance, I am convinced, must not be on a piecemeal basis as various crises develop. Any assistance that this Government may render in the future should provide a cure rather than a mere palliative. Any government that is willing to assist in the task of recovery will find full cooperation, I am sure, on the part of the United States Government. Any government which maneuvers to block the recovery of other countries cannot expect help from us. Furthermore, governments, political parties, or groups which seek to perpetuate human misery in order to profit therefrom politically or otherwise will encounter the opposition of the United States.

It is already evident that, before the United States Government can proceed much further in its efforts to alleviate the situation and help start the European world on its way to recovery, there must be some agreement among the countries of Europe as to the requirements of the situation and the part those countries themselves will take in order to give proper effect to whatever action might be undertaken by this Government. It would be neither fitting nor efficacious for this Government to undertake to draw up unilaterally a program designed to place

Europe on its feet economically. This is the business of the Europeans. The initiative, I think, must come from Europe. The role of this country should consist of friendly aid in the drafting of a European program and of later support of such a program so far as it may be practical for us to do so. The program should be a joint one, agreed to by a number, if not all, European nations.

An essential part of any successful action on the part of the United States is an understanding on the part of the people of America of the character of the problem and the remedies to be applied. Political passion and prejudice should have no part. With foresight, and a willingness on the part of our people to face up to the vast responsibility which history has clearly placed upon our country, the difficulties I have outlined can and will be overcome.

A Decade of American Foreign Policy, 1941–1949, pp. 1268-70

(c) *The North Atlantic Treaty Organization: Report of Secretary of State Dean G. Acheson to President Truman, April 7, 1949*

THE PRESIDENT: I have the honor to transmit to you the North Atlantic Treaty, signed at Washington on April 4, 1949, with the recommendation that it be submitted to the Senate for its advice and consent to ratification.

In accepting the obligations of the United Nations Charter in 1945, the United States Government committed itself for the first time to full participation in collective action to maintain international peace and security. The foreign policy of the United States is based squarely upon the United Nations as the primary instrument of international peace and progress. This Government is determined to make the United Nations ever more effective in order ultimately to assure universal peace.

Although this Government's full participation in world cooperation dates only from 1945, this Government had, for more than a century and a quarter, contributed to the peace of the Americas by making clear its determination to resist any attack upon our neighboring Republics to the South. The same determination and the obligations necessary to give it effect through the collective action of all the American Republics was incorporated in the Treaty of Rio de Janeiro in 1947. This Treaty, like the North Atlantic Treaty, is a defense arrangement under the Charter of the United Nations. The essence of that Treaty is recognition of the fact that an armed attack on any of the American States is in effect an attack upon them all.

The North Atlantic Treaty is patterned on the Treaty of Rio de Janeiro. Its essence is recognition of the fact that an armed attack on any of the North Atlantic nations is in effect an attack upon them all. An attack upon any of them would not be designed merely to gain territory or nationalistic ends. It would be directed squarely against our common democratic way of life.

The essential purpose of the Treaty is to fortify and preserve this common way of life. It is designed to contribute to the maintenance of peace by making clear in advance the determination of the Parties resolutely and collectively to resist armed attack on any of them. It is further designed to contribute to the stability and well-being of the member nations by removing the haunting sense of insecurity and enabling them to plan and work with confidence in the future. Finally, it is designed to provide the basis for effective collective action to restore and maintain the security of the North Atlantic area if an armed attack should occur.

This Treaty and the Rio Treaty, committing the United States as they do to exert its great influence for peace, are, in my opinion, second only in importance to our membership in the United Nations. For this reason every effort has been made to develop it on a wholly non-partisan basis and in cooperation between the Executive and Legislative branches.

In December 1947 you ratified the Treaty of Rio de Janeiro on the advice and consent of the Senate given with only one dissenting vote.

On March 17, 1948, the Governments of Belgium, France, Luxembourg, the Netherlands, and the United Kingdom signed the Brussels Treaty, which was modelled to a considerable extent on the Rio Treaty and which established another collective defense arrangement within the framework of the Charter. That arrangement was established with the encouragement of this Government as a step toward the closer integration of the free nations of Europe and as evidence of the determination of the five parties resolutely to defend themselves and each other against aggression. In establishing it, they repeatedly advised us that, despite their determination to do their utmost in self-defense, their collective strength might be inadequate to preserve peace or insure their national survival unless the great power and influence of the United States and other free nations were also brought into association with them.

On the day the Brussels Treaty was signed, you addressed the Congress in joint session and praised the conclusion of that Treaty as a notable step toward peace. You expressed confidence that the American people would extend to free countries the support which the situation might require and that their determination to defend themselves would be matched by an equal determination on our part to help them to do so.

Shortly thereafter, my predecessor, General Marshall, and Mr. Robert Lovett undertook a series of consultations with the leaders and members of the Senate Foreign Relations Committee on the problems facing the free world and how they might best be met by bringing American influence to bear in the cause of peace, in association with other free nations, and within the framework of the United Nations Charter.

On May 19, 1948, the Foreign Relations Committee unanimously reported Senate Resolution No. 239. That Resolution declared:

'WHEREAS peace with justice and the defense of human rights and fundamental freedoms require international cooperation through more effective use of the United Nations:

'Therefore be it

'RESOLVED, That the Senate reaffirm the policy of the United States to achieve international peace and security through the United Nations so that armed force shall not be used except in the common interest, and that the President be advised of the sense of the Senate that this Government, by constitutional process, should particularly pursue the following objectives within the United Nations Charter: . . .

'(2) Progressive development of regional and other collective arrangements for individual and collective self-defense in accordance with the purposes, principles, and provisions of the Charter.

'(3) Association of the United States, by constitutional process, with such regional and other collective arrangements as are based on continuous and effective self-help and mutual aid, and as affect its national security.

'(4) Contributing to the maintenance of peace by making clear its determination to exercise the right of individual or collective self-defense under Article 51 should any armed attack occur affecting its national security.'

On June 11, 1948, the Senate adopted that Resolution by a non-partisan vote of 64 to 4. The Preamble of H. R. 6802 which was unanimously reported by the Foreign Affairs Committee of the House of Representatives on June 9 but not voted upon prior to adjournment, contained language identical in substance with that quoted above.

In July, on the basis of these expressions of the wishes of the Legislative branch, you authorized Mr. Lovett to begin exploratory conversations with the Ambassadors of Canada and of the Parties to the Brussels Treaty. These conversations resulted in September in agreement by the representatives participating in them that an arrangement, established by Treaty, for the collective defense of the North Atlantic area was desirable and necessary. Agreement was also reached on the general nature of the Treaty. Following approval by the governments concerned of the recommendations of their representatives, negotiation of the Treaty was begun in December and finished on March 15, 1949.

Throughout these conversations and negotiations Mr. Lovett and I have constantly made clear that, so far as the United States was concerned, the Treaty must conform to the expression of guidance contained in the Senate Resolution. I am glad to say that the principles stated in the Resolution received the wholehearted concurrence of the other participating governments. From time to time during the negotiations first Mr. Lovett and, since January 20, I have consulted fully with the Chairman and ranking minority member of the Foreign Relations Committee. During the later stages of the negotiations I met twice with the Foreign Relations Committee as a whole. The Treaty in its final form reflects a number of constructive suggestions made by members of the Committee.

Early in March the Norwegian Government decided to join in negotiating the Treaty and since March 4 the Norwegian Ambassador has participated fully in the discussions.

It is clear that a collective defense arrangement of this nature, in order to be fully effective, should be participated in by as many countries as are in a position to further the democratic principles upon which the Treaty is based and to contribute to the security of the North Atlantic area and as are prepared to undertake the necessary responsibilities. Accordingly, invitations to become original signatories of the Treaty were issued on behalf of the eight participating governments on March 17 to the Governments of Denmark, Iceland, Italy, and Portugal. It is a source of gratification that those governments decided to participate in this collective enterprise.

Treaties are ordinarily negotiated in strict confidence and their contents made public only after signature. In this case, while it was necessary to conduct the negotiations in confidence until general agreement had been reached, the negotiating governments decided to make the text public as soon as it had been tentatively agreed upon. This was done in order to give public opinion in each of the participating countries and in all other countries the maximum opportunity to study and discuss its terms. I am exceedingly gratified by the popular reaction to the Treaty in the United States and abroad.

The text of the Treaty is, I think, self-explanatory. In drafting a document of such importance to millions of individuals every effort has been made to make it as clear, concise, and simple as possible. . . .

Article 3 carried into the Treaty the concept contained in the Senate Resolution that such collective arrangements should be based on continuous and effective self-help and mutual aid. This means that no Party can rely on others for its defense unless it does its utmost to defend itself and contribute toward the defense of the others. The Article does not itself obligate any Party to make any specific contribution to the defense capacity of any other Party, at any particular time or over any given period of time. It does contain the general obligations of determined self-defense and assistance in strengthening the defense capacity of the group as a whole. The concept of 'mutual aid' is that each Party shall contribute such mutual aid as it reasonably can, consistent with its geographic location and resources and with due regard to the requirements of basic economic health, in the form in which it can most effectively furnish it, whether in the form of facilities, manpower, productive capacity, military equipment, or other forms. . . .

Article 5 is based squarely on the 'inherent right', specifically recognized in Article 51 of the Charter, of 'individual or collective self-defense if an armed attack occurs against a member of the United Nations'. That right does not derive from Article 51 of the Charter; it is inherent, and recognized as such and preserved by that Article. The Article is also based upon the fact that in the world of today the security of the Parties to this Treaty is so interdependent that an armed attack on any one of them would be in effect an attack on all.

This Article provides that, if such an armed attack occurs, each Party will take such action as it deems necessary, including the use of armed force, to restore and maintain the security of the North Atlantic area.

The basic purpose of the Treaty is to contribute to the maintenance of peace, as recommended in the Senate Resolution, by making clear the determination of the Parties to exercise the right of self-defense should an armed attack occur against any of them. As you stated in your inaugural address, if it can be made sufficiently clear that such an attack would be met with overwhelming force, the attack may never occur.

This Treaty is designed to prevent such an attack occurring by making clear the determination of the signatory nations to take the necessary action should it occur. Far more important than language in a treaty is the determination of the peoples bound by it. It is my hope and belief that the American people and the peoples of the other signatory nations will by their national conduct make this unmistakably clear.

The obligation upon each Party is to use its honest judgment as to the action it deems necessary to restore and maintain the security of the North Atlantic area and accordingly to take such action as it deems necessary. Such action might or might not include the use of armed force depending upon the circumstances and gravity of the attack. If an attack were of a minor nature measures short of force would certainly be utilized first and might suffice. Only in the clear case of a major armed attack would the use of force be necessary. Each Party retains for itself the right of determination as to whether an armed attack has in fact occurred and what action it deems necessary to take. If the situation were not clear there would presumably be consultation prior to action. If the facts were clear, action would not necessarily depend on consultation and it is hoped that the action would be as swift and decisive as the gravity of the situation was deemed to require.

This does not mean that the United States would automatically be at war if we or one of the other Parties to the Treaty were attacked. Under our Constitution, the Congress alone has the power to declare war. The United States would be obligated by the Treaty to take promptly the action which it deemed necessary to restore and maintain the security of the North Atlantic area. That decision as to what action was necessary would naturally be taken in accordance with our constitutional processes.

Article 51 of the Charter recognizes the inherent right of self-defense until the Security Council has taken the measures necessary to maintain international peace and security. Article 5 of the Treaty provides that any armed attack upon a Party and all measures taken as a result thereof shall immediately be reported to the Security Council and that such measures shall be terminated when the Security Council has taken the necessary action. . . .

Article 13 provides that any Party may cease to be a Party, after the Treaty has been in force for 20 years, upon the expiration of one year's notice of denunciation.

The common heritage of the signatory nations dates deep in history and the bonds between them are fundamental. It is hoped that their cooperation will be permanent and progressively closer. The Treaty must have a relatively long duration if it is to provide the necessary assurance of long-term security and stability. On the other hand, the impossibility of foretelling what the international situation will be in the distant future makes rigidity for too long a term undesirable. It is believed that indefinite duration, with the possibility that any Party may withdraw from the Treaty after 20 years and that the Treaty as a whole might be reviewed at any time after it has been in effect for ten years, provides the best solution.

Article 14 is a formal article concerning the equal authenticity of the English and French texts and the disposition of the original Treaty and certified copies thereof.

I believe that this Treaty will prove to be an important milestone in realization of the desire of the American people to use their great influence for peace. It makes clear, in my opinion, their determination to do so. The Treaty has been formulated in accordance with the guidance given by the Senate in Resolution 239. In the Senate debate on that Resolution it was made clear that the Senate, in advising you particularly to pursue certain objectives, in no way yielded its freedom of action to scrutinize and to give or withhold its consent to ratification of such treaty as might be negotiated. I know that the Senate will conscientiously exercise that prerogative and I trust that the Treaty will meet with its approval.

A Decade of American Foreign Policy, 1941–1949, pp. 1332–9 (excerpts)

4 The Attack from the Left and the Right

(a) *Speech of Former Vice-President Henry A. Wallace, Madison Square Garden, New York City, March 31, 1947*

We are here tonight because we want peace.

We are here tonight because we mean to have peace.

We are here tonight to state that the Truman doctrine endangers peace.

We are here tonight to assert that peace requires Americans to reject that doctrine and reaffirm their faith in a strong United Nations.

Our soldiers did not win one war to fight another. Our workers and farmers toiled for freedom not for fear. Our dead did not bequeath to their children a legacy of death.

The world is hungry. The world cries out, not for American tanks and guns to destroy more lives and leave more hunger, but for American plows and food to fulfill the promise of peace.

The world is afraid. The world cries out, not for an American crusade in the name of hatred and fear of communism, but for a world crusade in the name of the brotherhood of man.

All of America's history was consecrated to that ideal. It was tested and proved in a great civil war. Twice in this generation Americans have fought for a free humanity. Today we come to a turning in freedom's road. Today America is in danger of turning aside.

In the name of crisis the President asks America to help the governments of Greece and Turkey.

In the name of crisis America is asked to ignore the world tribunal of the United Nations and take upon herself the role of prosecutor, judge, jury – and sheriff – what a role!

In the name of crisis facts are withheld, time is denied, hysteria is whipped up. The Congress is asked to rush through a momentous decision as if great armies were already on the march. I hear no armies marching. I hear a world crying out for peace. . . .

The welfare of all peoples is our concern. Famine anywhere endangers plenty everywhere. Progress anywhere helps progress everywhere. Action to help the world must help America. But not the action the President proposes. The needs of a desperate people are being exploited, just as the generosity of the Americans is being exploited – for other ends. The truth is that the President and his Republican backers are less concerned with the need of the Greek people for food than with the need of the American Navy for oil. The plan to contain communism is second to that need. For every glamorous admiral who boasts, it is 'Nobody's damn business where we go,' there are 10 drab but practical procurement officers to add, 'and we'll get there with Middle East oil.'

America is rich in oil but thinks she needs more for the greatest navy and air force in the world. When Britain competes for these resources, we settle our differences as friends. When Russia competes for them we sound a fire alarm and thank God for the atom bomb. Why? Great nations including Russia and America struggled for oil long before there were Communists in the Kremlin. Poverty, which causes communism, will be ended not by beating drums of hatred, but by world planning. I shall not blame America alone for present tensions, and I shall criticize Russia when I think Russia is wrong. But I do assert that a great part of our conflict with Russia is the normal conflict between two strong and sovereign nations and can be solved in normal ways. When some Americans assert that it is hopeless to seek an agreement with Russia on the Balkans and the Middle East, I answer, 'How do we know?' A program for United Nations development in the Balkans and Middle East has not been tried. . . .

The administration and its Republican supporters argue that we must intervene alone in Greece because the United Nations is too weak to act. I have not forgotten the appeasement of Hitler. I remember that every betrayal of world solidarity against Hitler by Daladier and Chamberlain was made in the name of the weakness of the League of Nations. Let us not betray the future. Let the world not destroy the United Nations as it once destroyed the League. . . .

There is but one hope for world peace – the United Nations. The Greek problem is a world problem and must be settled by the United Nations. If there is a Turkish problem, it, too, is the concern of all members of the United Nations. That is the spirit in which the Charter was signed.

We ask that the United Nations undertake a new program for relief of all peace-loving peoples in lands that have been devastated by war and today are in need. We ask that American funds be made available for this purpose.

We ask that the United Nations establish regional commissions for the reconstruction of Europe, the Middle East, and other areas as part of an over-all plan. To provide funds for reconstruction is the purpose of the World Bank. If the present Governors of the Bank are unwilling to act, then the Bank should be given Governors who will act. Adequate funds should be made available to support the Bank.

We ask that the United Nations face the problem of security not piecemeal but on a world-wide basis. This means the internationalization of the Dardanelles, the Suez Canal, and the Panama Canal. It means world disarmament and world control of atomic energy. It means real assurance against aggression and also adequate provision for peaceful change.

Let us do for the United Nations what needs to be done to carry out these tasks.

If the United Nations is untested, let us test it.

If the United Nations lacks support, let us support it.

If the United Nations is weak, let us strengthen it.

No one pretends that the United Nations will meet all needs and solve all problems overnight.

Patience and toil will not give us the millennium, but they will help to make a more decent world than we have ever known.

If we reject this course, the United Nations will crumble and man's hope will perish. Sooner or later Truman's program of unconditional aid to anti-Soviet governments will unite the world against America and divide America against herself.

The Truman program must turn the world against America. At our command freedom, in whose name Americans have died, will become a catchword for reaction. Once we grant unconditional loans to the undemocratic Governments of Greece and Turkey, then, in the name of freedom, every Fascist dictator will know that he has credit in our bank. Today it is the Governments of Greece and Turkey. Tomorrow it may be Peron and Chiang Kai-shek. Our banks will give dollars; our arsenals will give weapons. When that is not enough our people will be asked to give their sons.

The Truman program must turn Americans against each other. It will threaten everything in America that is worth fighting for. Intolerance is aroused. Suspicion is engendered. Men of the highest integrity in public life are besmirched. The President's Executive order creates a master index of public servants. From the janitor in the village post office to the Cabinet member, they are to be sifted and tested and watched and appraised. Their past and present, the tattle and prattle of their neighbors, are all to be recorded. But more Americans than these are in danger of persecution. . . .

Hatred and violence abroad, hatred and fear at home will be the fruits of the Truman doctrine. A strong United Nations can bring peace. Which do we choose – for America must choose. The world waits for the American people.

Where are the millions who supported Roosevelt's ideals? Where are the inheritors of our great tradition? In weariness and confusion many Americans have abandoned political action. Now they must return. Their country needs them. Americans of all parties, all faiths, all creeds must now speak out in one great voice for peace and freedom.

America is our country. Because we love America, because we want America to be free and at peace in a world free and at peace, we say:

No imperialist adventures. Support the United Nations.

Millions to feed the hungry. Not one cent to arm tyranny.

Down with intolerance and bigotry. Back to the faith of our fathers.

Congressional Record, Senate, 80th Congress, 1st Session, Appendix, April 9, 1947, pp. A1572–3 (as read into the record by Senator Glen Taylor)

(b) *McCarthyism: The Attack on the Department of State. Senator McCarthy's Speech at Wheeling, West Virginia in February, 1950, as later repeated on the floor of the U.S. Senate, February 20, 1950*

. . . Today we are engaged in a final, all-out battle between communistic atheism and Christianity. The modern champions of communism have selected this as the time. And, ladies and gentlemen, the chips are down – they are truly down. . . .

Ladies and gentlemen, can there be anyone here tonight who is so blind as to say that the war is not on? Can there be anyone who fails to realize that the Communist world has said, 'The time is now – that this is the time for the show-down between the democratic Christian world and the Communist atheistic world?

Unless we face this fact, we shall pay the price that must be paid by those who wait too long.

Six years ago, at the time of the first conference to map out the peace – Dumbarton Oaks – there was within the Soviet orbit 180,000,000 people. Lined up on the antitotalitarian side there were in the world at that time roughly 1,625,000,000 people. Today, only 6 years later, there are 800,000,000 people under the absolute domination of Soviet Russia – an increase of over 400 percent. On our side, the figure has shrunk to around 500,000,000. In other words, in less than 6 years the odds have changed from 9 to 1 in our favor to 8 to 5 against us. This indicates the swiftness of the tempo of Communist victories and American defeats in the cold war. As one of our outstanding historical figures once said, 'When a great democracy is destroyed, it will not be because of enemies from without, but rather because of enemies from within.'

The truth of this statement is becoming terrifyingly clear as we see this country each day losing on every front.

At war's end we were physically the strongest nation on earth and, at least potentially, the most powerful intellectually and morally. Ours could have been the honor of being a beacon in the desert of destruction, a shining living proof that civilization was not yet ready to destroy itself. Unfortunately, we have failed miserably and tragically to arise to the opportunity.

The reason why we find ourselves in a position of impotency is not because our only powerful potential enemy has sent men to invade our shores, but rather because of the traitorous actions of those who have been treated so well by this Nation. It has not been the less fortunate or members of minority groups who have been selling this Nation out, but rather those who have had all the benefits that the wealthiest nation on earth has had to offer – the finest homes, the finest college education, and the finest jobs in Government we can give.

This is gloriously true in the State Department. There the bright young men who are born with silver spoons in their mouths are the ones who have been worst. . . .

This, ladies and gentlemen, gives you somewhat of a picture of the type of individuals who have been helping to shape our foreign policy. In my opinion the State Department, which is one of the most important government departments, is thoroughly infested with Communists.

I have in my hand 57 cases of individuals who would appear to be either card carrying members or certainly loyal to the Communist Party, but who nevertheless are still helping to shape our foreign policy.

One thing to remember in discussing the Communists in our Government is that we are not dealing with spies who get 30 pieces of silver to steal the blueprints of a new weapon. We are dealing with a far more sinister type of activity because it permits the enemy to guide and shape our policy.

Congressional Record, Senate, 81st Congress, 2nd Session, February 20, 1950, pp. 1954–55

5 The China Tangle

Letter from Secretary of State Dean Acheson to President Truman, transmitting 'United States Relations with China, with Special Reference to the Period 1944–1949', July 30, 1949

THE PRESIDENT: In accordance with your wish, I have had compiled a record of our relations with China, special emphasis being placed on the last five years. This record is being published and will therefore be available to the Congress and to the people of the United States. . . .

The reasons for the failures of the Chinese National Government appear in some detail in the attached record. They do not stem from any inadequacy of American aid. Our military observers on the spot have reported that the Nationalist armies did not lose a single battle during the crucial year of 1948 through lack of arms or ammunition. The fact was that the decay which our observers had detected in Chungking early in the war had fatally sapped the powers of resistance of the Kuomintang. Its leaders had proved incapable of meeting the crisis confronting them, its troops had lost the will to fight, and its Government had lost popular support. The Communists, on the other hand, through a ruthless discipline and fanatical zeal, attempted to sell themselves as guardians and liberators of the people. The Nationalist armies did not have to be defeated; they disintegrated. History has proved again and again that a regime without faith in itself and an army without morale cannot survive the test of battle.

The record obviously can not set forth in equal detail the inner history and development of the Chinese Communist Party during these years. The principal reason is that, while we had regular diplomatic relations with the National Government and had the benefit of voluminous reports from our representatives in their territories, our direct contact with the Communists was limited in the main to the mediation efforts of General Hurley and General Marshall.

Fully recognizing that the heads of the Chinese Communist Party were ideologically affiliated with Moscow, our Government nevertheless took the view, in the light of the existing balance of forces in China, that peace could be established only if certain conditions were met. The Kuomintang would have to set its own house in order and both sides would have to make concessions so that the Government of China might become, in fact as well as in name, the Government of all China and so that all parties might function within the constitutional system of the Government. Both internal peace and constitutional development required that the progress should be rapid from one party government with a large opposition party in armed rebellion, to the participation of all parties, including the moderate non-communist elements, in a truly national system of government.

None of these conditions has been realized. The distrust of the leaders of both the Nationalist and Communist Parties for each other proved too deep-seated to permit final agreement, notwithstanding temporary truces and apparently promising negotiations. The Nationalists, furthermore, embarked in 1946 on an over-ambitious military campaign in the face of warnings by General Marshall that it not only would fail but would plunge China into economic chaos and eventually destroy the National Government. General Marshall pointed out that though Nationalist armies could, for a period, capture Communist-held cities, they could not destroy the Communist armies. Thus every Nationalist advance would expose their communications to attack by Communist guerrillas and compel them to retreat or to surrender their armies together with the munitions which the United States has furnished them. No estimate of a military situation has ever been more completely confirmed by the resulting facts.

The historic policy of the United States of friendship and aid toward the people of China was, however, maintained in both peace and war. Since V–J Day, the United States Government has authorized aid to Nationalist China in the form of grants and credits totalling approximately 2 billion dollars, an amount equivalent in value to more than 50 percent of the monetary expenditures of the Chinese Government and of proportionately greater magnitude in relation to the budget of that Government than the United States has provided to any nation of Western Europe since the end of the war. In addition to these grants and credits, the United States Government has sold the Chinese Government large quantities of military and civilian war surplus property with a total procurement cost of over 1 billion dollars, for which the agreed realization to the United States was 232 million dollars. A large proportion of the military supplies furnished the Chinese armies by the United States since V–J Day has, however, fallen into the hands of the Chinese Communists through the military ineptitude of the Nationalist leaders, their defections and surrenders, and the absence among their forces of the will to fight.

It has been urged that relatively small amounts of additional aid – military and economic – to the National Government would have enabled it to destroy communism in China. The most trustworthy military, economic, and political information available to our Government does not bear out this view.

A realistic appraisal of conditions in China, past and present, leads to the conclusion that the only alternative open to the United States was full-scale intervention in behalf of a Government which had lost the confidence of its own troops and its own people. Such intervention would have required the expenditure of even greater sums than have been fruitlessly spent thus far, the command of Nationalist armies by American officers, and the probable participation of American armed forces – land, sea, and air – in the resulting war. Intervention of such a scope and magnitude would have been resented by the mass of the Chinese people, would have diametrically reversed our historic policy, and would have been condemned by the American people.

It must be admitted frankly that the American policy of assisting the Chinese people in resisting domination by any foreign power or powers is now confronted with the gravest difficulties. The heart of China is in Communist hands. The Communist leaders have foresworn their Chinese heritage and have publicly announced their subservience to a foreign power, Russia, which during the last 50 years, under czars and Communists alike, has been most assiduous in its efforts to extend its control in the Far East. In the recent past, attempts at foreign domination have appeared quite clearly to the Chinese people as external aggression and as such have been bitterly and in the long run successfully resisted. Our aid and encouragement have helped them to resist. In this case, however, the foreign domination has been masked behind the facade of a vast crusading movement which apparently has seemed to many Chinese to be wholly indigenous and national. Under these circumstances, our aid has been unavailing.

The unfortunate but inescapable fact is that the ominous result of the civil war in China was beyond the control of the government of the United States. Nothing that this country did or could have done within the reasonable limits of its capabilities could have changed that result; nothing that was left undone by this country has contributed to it. It was the product of internal Chinese forces, forces which this country tried to influence but could not. A decision was arrived at within China, if only a decision by default.

And now it is abundantly clear that we must face the situation as it exists in fact. We will not help the Chinese or ourselves by basing our policy on wishful thinking. We continue to believe that, however tragic may be the immediate future of China and however ruthlessly a major portion of this great people may be exploited by a party in the interest of a foreign imperialism, ultimately the profound civilization and the democratic individualism of China will reassert themselves and she will throw off the foreign yoke. I consider that we should encourage all developments in China which now and in the future work toward this end.

In the immediate future, however, the implementation of our historic policy of friendship for China must be profoundly affected by current developments. It will necessarily be influenced by the degree to which the Chinese people come to recognize that the Communist regime serves not their interests but those of Soviet Russia and the manner in which, having become aware of the facts, they react to this foreign domination. One point, however, is clear. Should the Communist regime lend itself to the aims of Soviet Russian imperialism and attempt to engage in aggression against China's neighbors, we and the other members of the United Nations would be confronted by a situation violative of the principles of the United Nations Charter and threatening international peace and security.

Meanwhile our policy will continue to be based upon our own

respect for the Charter, our friendship for China, and our traditional support for the Open Door and for China's independence and administrative and territorial integrity.

A Decade of American Foreign Policy, pp. 715-26 (excerpts)

6 Korea and MacArthur

(a) *Address by General Douglas MacArthur to a Joint Session of Congress, April 19, 1951*

. . . I address you with neither rancor nor bitterness in the fading twilight of life with but one purpose in mind: to serve my country.

The issues are global and so interlocked that to consider the problems of one sector, oblivious to those of another, is but to court disaster for the whole.

While Asia is commonly referred to as the gateway to Europe, it is no less true that Europe is the gateway to Asia, and the broad influence of the one cannot fail to have its impact upon the other. There are those who claim our strength is inadequate to protect on both fronts, that we can not divide our effort. I can think of no greater expression of defeatism.

If a potential enemy can divide his strength on two fronts, it is for us to counter his effort. The Communist threat is a global one. Its successful advance in one sector threatens the destruction of every other sector. You cannot appease or otherwise surrender to Communism in Asia without simultaneously undermining our efforts to halt its advance in Europe. . . .

While I was not consulted prior to the President's decision to intervene in support of the Republic of Korea, that decision, from a military standpoint, proved a sound one. As I say, it proved a sound one, as we hurled back the invader and decimated his forces. Our victory was complete and our objectives within reach when Red China intervened with numerically superior ground forces.

This created a new war and an entirely new situation, a situation not contemplated when our forces were committed against the North Korean invaders, a situation which called for new decisions in the diplomatic sphere to permit the realistic adjustment of military strategy.

Such decisions have not been forthcoming.

While no man in his right mind would advocate sending our ground forces into continental China, and such was never given a thought, the new situation did urgently demand a drastic revision of strategic planning if our political aim was to defeat this new enemy as we had defeated the old.

Apart from the military need, as I saw it, to neutralize the sanctuary protection given the enemy north of Yalu, I felt that military necessity in the conduct of the war made necessary, first, the intensification of our economic blockade against China; second, the imposition of a naval blockade against the China coast; third, removal of restrictions on air reconnaissance of China's coastal areas and of Manchuria; fourth, removal of restrictions on the forces of the Republic of China on Formosa with logistical support to contribute to their effective operations against the Chinese mainland.

For entertaining these views, all professionally designed to support our forces committed to Korea and bring hostilities to an end with the least possible delay at a saving of countless American and Allied lives, I have been severely criticized in lay circles, principally abroad, despite my understanding that from a military standpoint the above views have been fully shared in the past by practically every military leader concerned with the Korean campaign, including our own Joint Chiefs of Staff.

I called for reinforcements, but was informed that reinforcements were not available. I made clear that, if not permitted to destroy the enemy-built-up bases north of the Yalu, if not permitted to utilize the friendly Chinese force of some 600,000 men on Formosa, if not permitted to blockade the China coast to prevent the Chinese Reds from getting succor from without, and if there were to be no hope of major reinforcements, the position of the command from the military standpoint forbade victory.

We could hold in Korea by constant maneuver, and at an approximate area where our supply-line advantages were in balance with the supply-line disadvantages of the enemy. But we could hope at best for only an indecisive campaign with its terrible and constant attrition upon our forces if the enemy utilized his full military potential.

I have constantly called for the new political decisions essential to a solution. Efforts have been made to distort my position. It has been said in effect that I was a warmonger. Nothing could be further from the truth. . . .

But once war is forced upon us, there is no other alternative than to apply every available means to bring it to a swift end. War's very object is victory, not prolonged indecision.

In war there is no substitute for victory. There are some who, for varying reasons, would appease Red China. They are blind to history's clear lesson, for history teaches, with unmistakable emphasis, that appeasement but begets new and bloodier war. It points to no single instance where this end has justified that means, where appeasement has led to more than a sham peace. Like blackmail, it lays the basis for new and successively greater demands until, as in blackmail, violence becomes the only other alternative. Why, my soldiers asked of me, surrender military advantages to an enemy in the field? I could not answer.

Some may say to avoid spread of the conflict into an all-out war with China. Others, to avoid Soviet intervention. Neither explanation seems valid, for China is already engaging with the maximum power it can commit, and the Soviet will not necessarily mesh its actions with our moves. Like a cobra, any new enemy will more likely strike whenever it feels that the relativity in military or other potential is in its favor on a world-wide basis.

The tragedy of Korea is further heightened by the fact that its military action is confined to its territorial limits. It condemns that nation, which it is our purpose to save, to suffer the devastating impact of full naval and air bombardment while the enemy's sanctuaries are fully protected from such attack and devastation.

Of the nations of the world, Korea alone, up to now, is the sole one which has risked its all against communism. The magnificence of the courage and fortitude of the Korean people defies description. They have chosen to risk death rather than slavery. Their last words to me were: 'Don't scuttle the Pacific.'

I am closing my fifty-two years of military service. When I joined the Army, even before the turn of the century, it was the fulfillment of all my boyish hopes and dreams.

The world has turned over many times since I took the oath on the plain at West Point, and the hopes and dreams have long since vanished, but I still remember the refrain of one of the most popular barracks ballads of that day which proclaimed most proudly that old soldiers never die; they just fade away.

And like the old soldier of that ballad, I now close my military career and just fade away, an old soldier who tried to do his duty as God gave him the light to see that duty. Good bye.

Congressional Record, House of Representatives, 82nd Congress, 1st Session, April 19, 1951, pp. 4123-5

(b) *Opening Statement of General Omar Bradley, Chairman of the Joint Chiefs of Staff, before the Armed Forces and Foreign Relations Committees of the Senate, May 15, 1951*

. . . Before your interrogation on the details of our Government's policies in Korea and the Far East, I would like to ask myself this question: What is the great issue at stake in this hearing?

Principally I would say that you are trying to determine the course we should follow as the best road to peace. There are military factors which must be evaluated before a sound decision can be made. At present the issue is obscured in the public mind by many details which do not relate to the task of keeping the peace and making America secure.

The fundamental military issue that has arisen is whether to increase the risk of a global war by taking additional measures that are open to the United States and its allies. We now have a localized conflict in Korea. Some of the military measures under discussion might well place the United States in the position of responsibility for broadening the war and at the same time losing most if not all of our allies.

General MacArthur has stated that there are certain additional measures which can and should be taken, and that by so doing no unacceptable increased risk of global war will result.

The Joint Chiefs of Staff believe that these same measures do increase the risk of global war and that such a risk should not be taken unnecessarily. At the same time we recognize the military advantages that might accrue to the United Nations' position in Korea and to the United States position in the Far East by these measures. While a field commander very properly estimates his needs from the viewpoint of operations in his own theatre or sphere of action, those responsible for higher direction must necessarily base their actions on broader aspects, and on the needs, actual or prospective, of several theatres.

The Joint Chiefs of Staff, in view of their global responsibilities and their perspective with respect to the world-wide strategic situation, are in a better position than is any single theatre commander to assess the risk of general war. Moreover, the Joint Chiefs of Staff are best able to judge our own military resources with which to meet that risk.

In order that all may understand the strategy which the Joint Chiefs of Staff believe the United States must pursue, I would like to discuss in broad terms this perspective in which we view our security problems. . . .

We must understand – as we conduct our foreign affairs and our military affairs – that while power and nationalism prevail, it is up to us to gain strength through cooperative efforts with other nations which have common ideals and objectives with our own. At the same time, we must create and maintain the power essential to persuasion, and to our own security in such a world. We must understand the role and nature, including the limitations, of this power if we are to exercise it wisely.

One of the great power potentials of this world is the United States of America and her allies. The other great power in this world is Soviet Russia and her satellites. As much as we desire peace, we must realize that we have two centers of power supporting opposing ideologies.

From a global viewpoint – and with the security of our nation of prime importance – our military mission is to support a policy of preventing communism from gaining the manpower, the resources, the raw material and the industrial capacity essential to world domination. If Soviet Russia ever controls the entire Eurasian land mass, then the Soviet-satellite imperialism may have the broad base upon which to build the military power to rule the world.

Three times in the past five years the Kremlin-inspired imperialism has been thwarted by direct action.

In Berlin, Greece and Korea the free nations have opposed Communist aggression with a different type of action. But each time the power of the United States had been called upon and we have become involved. Each incident has cost us money, resources and some lives.

But in each instance we have prevented the domination of one more area and the absorption of another source of manpower, raw materials and resources.

Korea, in spite of the importance of the engagement, must be looked upon with proper perspective. It is just one engagement, just one phase of this battle that we are having with the other power center in the world which opposes us and all we stand for. For five years this 'guerrilla diplomacy' has been going on. In each of the actions in which we have participated to oppose this gangster conduct we have risked World War III. But each time we have used methods short of total war. As costly as Berlin and Greece and Korea may be, they are less expensive than the vast destruction which would be inflicted upon all sides if a total war were to be precipitated.

I am under no illusion that our present strategy of using means short of total war to achieve our ends and oppose communism is a guarantee that a world war will not be thrust upon us. But a policy of patience and determination without provoking world war, while we improve our military power, is one which we believe we must continue to follow.

As long as we keep the conflict within its present scope, we are holding to a minimum the forces we must commit and tie down.

The strategic alternative, enlargement of the war in Korea to include Red China, would probably delight the Kremlin more than anything else we could do. It would necessarily tie down additional forces, especially our sea power and our air power, while the Soviet Union would not be obliged to put a single man into the conflict.

Under the present circumstances, we have recommended against enlarging the war. The course of action often described as a 'limited war' with Red China would increase the risk we are taking by engaging too much of our power in an area that is not the critical strategic prize.

Red China is not the powerful nation seeking to dominate the world. Frankly, in the opinion of the Joint Chiefs of Staff, this strategy would involve us in the wrong war, at the wrong place, at the wrong time and with the wrong enemy. . . .

Hearings before the Committee on the Armed Forces and the Committee on Foreign Relations (Washington, 1951), Part II, pp. 729-31 (82nd Congress, 1st Session)

7 The Republican View

Excerpts from an article in 'Life Magazine' by John Foster Dulles, May 19, 1952

Soviet Communism confronts our nation with its gravest peril. To meet its long-term strategy of encirclement and strangulation, we have adopted a series of emergency measures which are fantastically costly not only in money but in their warping of our American way of life.

No one would begrudge the cost of what we are doing if, in fact, it was adequate and was ending the peril, and if there was no better way. Actually, our policies are *inadequate* in scope. They are *not* ending the peril. There *is* a better way.

II

The costs of our present policies are perilously high in money, in freedom and in friendships.

The Administration's 'security policies' would this year cost us, in money, about 60 billion, of which about 99% goes for military purposes and for equipment (which will quickly become obsolete and demand replacement indefinitely). Such gigantic expenditures unbalance our budget and require taxes so heavy that they discourage incentive. They so cheapen the dollar that savings, pensions and Social Security reserves have already lost much of their value.

What is worse, this concentration on military matters is – to use George Washington's words – 'inauspicious to liberty'. It leads to encroachments on civil rights and transfers from the civilian to the military decisions which profoundly affect our domestic life and our foreign relations.

We are also rapidly expending our friendships and prestige in the world. Increasing numbers turn away from our policies as too militaristic, too costly, too erratic and too inconclusive for them to follow. Our far-flung, extravagant and surreptitious military projects are frightening many who feel that we are conducting a private feud with Russia, which may endanger them, rather than performing a public service for peace.

All these are, indeed, perilously high costs.

There are times when nations have to pay such costs to win a victory and end a peril. We know that from the last two World Wars. But today our policies are not designed to win a victory conclusively.

If you will think back over the past six years, you will see that our policies have largely involved emergency action to try to 'contain' Soviet Communism by checking it here or blocking it there. We are not working, sacrificing and spending in order to be able to live *without* this peril – but to be able to live *with* it, presumably forever. . . .

In all these matters our actions were merely reactions to some of the many Soviet threats. As such, they have been reasonably successful. But that is only a small part of the story. Since 1945, when World War II fighting ended, the Soviet Communists have won control over all or parts of 12 countries in Asia and Central Europe with populations of about 600 million. Their mood today is one of triumphant expectancy: 'Which will be the next addition to our camp?' The free world is full of foreboding: 'Which of us will be the next victim?'

Our present negative policies will never end the type of sustained offensive which Soviet Communism is mounting; they will never end the peril nor bring relief from the exertions which devour our economic, political and moral vitals. Ours are treadmill policies which, at best, might perhaps keep us in the same place until we drop exhausted.

As former Ambassador Minocher R. Masani of India recently put the matter tersely: 'Defenses seem constantly improvised' – a hole plugged here, a leak stopped there. . . . Clearly, mere containment is no longer enough.' . . .

III

Where do we go from here? . . .

There are a few Republicans – and some Democrats – who would turn their backs on all the world's problems and wrap the United States in some magically 'impregnable' isolation.

Such policies would really give 100% cooperation to the Soviet Communist effort to encircle and isolate us, as a preliminary to a final assault. Once Asia, Europe, Africa and probably South America were consolidated against us, our plight would be desperate.

The mere fact that such a retreat is seriously discussed shows that the frustration of past hopes is inducing a somewhat morbid state of mind which minimizes our assets pathetically and exaggerates those of Soviet Communism ludicrously. It assumes we are *lacking* strength rather than that we are *misusing* it.

Looked at in any impartial way, we are the world's greatest and strongest power. The only commodity in which we seem deficient is faith. In all material things we have a productivity far exceeding that of Russia: our steel production is about three and one half times that of the Soviet Union, and in aluminum, petroleum and electric power our superiority is even greater. Our people have a standard of education, an inventive talent and a technical skill unmatched by any of the peoples under Soviet rule.

On the Soviet side a dozen people in the Kremlin are attempting to rule 800 million human beings – while trying to conquer more. All except a privileged few work under conditions which sternly deny them the 'pursuit of happiness.' Within Russia itself the discontent can be judged by the 15 million prisoners in forced labor camps – more than twice the membership of the Soviet Communist party. Even the leaders are suspicious of each other as each wonders whether the other plots his purge. . . .

IV

As we stop fretting and start thinking, the first problem to tackle is the strictly military one. It comes in the form of a paradox: for we must seek a military formula more effective than any devised to date –

that we may no longer be so overridingly preoccupied with purely military necessity. . . .

Those who think only of Western Europe and of making it 'impregnable' – without regard to the Near, Middle and Far East and Africa – are just as blind as those who think only of the United States and of making it 'impregnable'. Policies that do not defend freedom in Asia are fatally defective.

How do we defend it? Obviously, we cannot build a 20,000-mile Maginot Line or match the Red armies, man for man, gun for gun and tank for tank at any particular time or place their general staff selects. To attempt that would mean real strength nowhere and bankruptcy everywhere.

There is one solution and only one: that is for the free world to develop the will and organize the means to retaliate instantly against open aggression by Red armies, so that, if it occurred anywhere, we could and would strike back where it hurts, by means of our choosing.

The principle involved is as simple as that of our municipal police forces. We do not station armed guards at every house to stop aggressors – that would be economic suicide – but we deter potential aggressors by making it probable that if they aggress, they will lose in punishment more than they can gain by aggression.

By analogy the free world, for its common defense, needs community punishing power. It could consist of:

(1) The creation, at whatever are the convenient places, of means to hit with shattering effectiveness the sources of power and lines of communication of the Sovietized world;

(2) The determination in advance, by common consent given by constitutional and United Nations processes, that this power would be used instantly if, but only if, the Red armies of the Soviet Union or its satellites, including China, engage in open armed attack;

(3) The continuous maintenance of observers along the frontiers enjoying protection, who would immediately report if such armed aggression occurred. The United Nations Peace Observation Commission, or some comparable body, could supply these observers.

Such a community punishing power could conclusively deter open armed aggression. To argue timidly that it would provoke such aggression is to ignore the facts. The plainest of these facts is that the Kremlin has not used its Red armies for open military conquest even in these past years when there were no military obstacles in their path. The truth is that there are sound reasons why the Soviet leaders have not used – and may not use – their armies in open aggression. . . .

The cumulative weight of these deterrents has proved great. It could be made overwhelming by the creation of a community punish-force known to be ready and resolute to retaliate, in the event of any armed aggression, with *weapons* of its choosing against *targets* of its choosing at *times* of its choosing.

Today atomic energy, coupled with strategic air and sea power, provides the community of free nations with vast new possibilities of organizing a community power to stop open aggression before it starts and reduce, to the vanishing point, the risk of general war. So far these weapons are merely part of national arsenals for use in fighting general war when it has come. If that catastrophe occurs, it will be because we have allowed these new and awesome forces to become the ordinary killing tools of the soldier when, in the hands of the statesmen, they could serve as effective political weapons in defense of the peace.

V

Once the free world has established a military defense, it can undertake what has been too long delayed – a political offense.

It is ironic and wrong that we who believe in the boundless power of human freedom should so long have accepted a static political role. It is also ironic and wrong that we who so proudly profess regard for the spiritual should rely so utterly on material defenses while the avowed materialists have been waging a winning war with social ideas, stirring humanity everywhere.

There are three truths which we need to recall in these times:

1) The dynamic prevails over the static; the active over the passive. We were from the beginning a vigorous, confident people, born with a sense of destiny and of mission. That is why we have grown from a small and feeble nation to our present stature in the world.

2) Nonmaterial forces are more powerful than those that are merely material. Our dynamism has always been moral and intellectual rather than military or material. During most of our national life we had only a small military establishment and during the last century we had to borrow money abroad to develop our expanding economy. But we always generated political, social and industrial ideas and projected them abroad where they were more explosive than dynamite.

3) There is a moral or natural law not made by man which determines right and wrong and in the long run only those who conform to that law will escape disaster. This law has been trampled by the Soviet rulers, and for that violation they can and should be made to

pay. This will happen when we ourselves keep faith with that law in our practical decisions of policy.

We should let these truths work in and through us. We should be *dynamic*, we should use *ideas* as weapons; and these ideas should conform to *moral* principles. That we do this is right, for it is the inevitable expression of a faith – and I am confident that we still do have a faith. But it is also expedient in defending ourselves against an aggressive, imperialistic despotism. For even the present lines will not hold unless our purpose goes beyond confining Soviet Communism within its present orbit.

Consider the situation of the 20-odd non-Western nations which are next door to the Soviet world. These exposed nations feel that they have been put in the 'expendable' class, condemned in perpetuity to be the ramparts against which the angry waves of Soviet Communism will constantly hurl themselves. They are expected to live precariously, permanently barred from areas with which they normally should have trade, commerce and cultural relations. They cannot be enthusiastic about policies which would merely perpetuate so hazardous and uncomfortable a position. Today they live close to despair because the United States, the historic leader of the forces of freedom, seems dedicated to the negative policy of 'containment' and 'stalemate'.

As a matter of fact some highly competent work is being done, at one place or another, to promote liberation. Obviously such activities do not lend themselves to public exposition. But liberation from the yoke of Moscow will not occur for a very long time, and courage in neighboring lands will not be sustained, *unless the United States makes it publicly known that it wants and expects liberation to occur*. The mere statement of that wish and expectation would change, in an electrifying way, the mood of the captive peoples. It would put heavy new burdens on the jailers and create new opportunities for liberation.

Here are some specific acts which we could take:

1) We could make it clear, on the highest authority of the President and the Congress, that U.S. policy seeks as one of its peaceful goals the eventual restoration of genuine independence in the nations of Europe and Asia now dominated by Moscow, and that we will not be a party to any 'deal' confirming the rule of Soviet despotism over the alien peoples which it now dominates.

2) We could welcome the creation in the free world of political 'task forces' to develop a freedom program for each of the captive nations. Each group would be made up of those who are proved

patriots, who have practical resourcefulness and who command confidence and respect at home and abroad.

3) We could stimulate the escape from behind the Iron Curtain of those who can help to develop these programs.

4) The activities of the Voice of America and such private committees as those for Free Europe and Free Asia could be coordinated with these freedom programs. The agencies would be far more effective if given concrete jobs to do.

5) We could coordinate our economic, commercial and cultural relations with the freedom programs, cutting off or licensing intercourse as seemed most effective from time to time.

6) We could end diplomatic relations with present governments which are in fact only puppets of Moscow, if and when that would promote the freedom programs.

7) We could seek to bring other free nations to unite with us in proclaiming, in a great new Declaration of Independence, our policies toward the captive nations.

We do not want a series of bloody uprisings and reprisals. There can be peaceful separation from Moscow, as Tito showed, and enslavement can be made so unprofitable that the master will let go his grip. Such results will not come to pass overnight. But we can know, for history proves, that the spirit of patriotism burns unquenched in Poles, Czechs, Hungarians, Romanians, Bulgarians, Chinese and others, and we can be confident that within two, five or 10 years substantial parts of the present captive world can peacefully regain national independence. That will mark the beginning of the end of Soviet despotism's attempt at world conquest. . . .

VIII

The ideas expressed here are not put forward dogmatically but to stimulate discussion on problems so difficult that the wisest men can disagree. But on two points I do venture to be dogmatic. First: we must move promptly to get out of the present morass. Second: the policies that get us out must reflect the basic qualities that have made our nation great in the best sense of that ambiguous word.

This nation was founded by men of lofty purpose. They were not content merely to build here a snug haven but they sought to create a political system which would inspire just government throughout the world. Our Declaration of Independence, as Lincoln said, meant 'liberty, not alone for the people of this country, but hope to all the world, for all future time.' We have always been, as we always should be, the despair of the oppressor and the hope of the oppressed. . . .

The policies I have here put forward seek to meet these traditional tests. They would recommit our nation to the universal cause of human liberty and just government. They would commit our offensive military power to the deterring of aggression and the preservation of peace.

These policies, I believe, do even more than bespeak those enduring principles that are our priceless spiritual heritage. They befit our nation in its majestic role today – at once the guardian and the servant of the hopes of all who love freedom.

John Foster Dulles, 'A Policy of Boldness', *Life* (May 19, 1952), Vol. 32, No. 20, pp. 146-160 (excerpts)

SELECT BIBLIOGRAPHY

The best general text is Leopold, Richard W., *The Growth of American Foreign Policy* (New York: Knopf, 1963)

Adler, Selig, *The Isolationist Impulse* (New York: Abelard-Schuman, 1957)
Burns, James, *Roosevelt: The Lion and the Fox* (New York: Harcourt, 1956)
Davison, Walter, *The Berlin Blockade* (Princeton: Princeton Univ. Press, 1958)
Divine, Robert, *Second Chance* (New York: Athenaeum, 1967)
Feis, Herbert, *The Road to Pearl Harbor* (Princeton: Princeton Univ. Press, 1950)
Feis, Herbert, *Churchill, Roosevelt, Stalin* (Princeton: Princeton Univ. Press, 1957)
Feis, Herbert, *1933 – Characters in Crisis* (Boston: Little-Brown, 1966)
Ferrell, Robert, *Peace in Their Time* (New Haven: Yale Univ. Press, 1952)
Ferrell, Robert, *American Diplomacy in the Great Depression* (New Haven: Yale Univ. Press, 1957)
Goold-Adams, Richard, *John Foster Dulles: A Reappraisal* (New York: Appleton-Century Crofts, 1962)
Greenfield, Kent, *American Strategy in World War II: A Reconsideration* (Baltimore: Johns Hopkins Univ. Press, 1963)
Halle, Louis, *The Cold War as History* (New York: Harper and Row, 1967)
Iriye, Akira, *After Imperialism* (Cambridge: Harvard Univ. Press, 1965)
Jones, Joseph, *The Fifteen Weeks* (New York: Viking, 1955)
Kennan, George, *Russia and the West under Lenin and Stalin* (Boston: Little-Brown, 1961)
Kennan, George, *Memoirs, 1925–1950* (Boston: Little-Brown, 1967)
LaFeber, Walter, *America, Russia, and the Cold War* (New York, Wiley, 1967)
Langer, William L., and Gleason, Everett, *The Challenge to Isolation* and *The Undeclared War* (New York: Council on Foreign Relations, 1952 and 1953)
McNeill, W. H., *America, Britain, and Russia: Their Cooperation and Conflict* (London: Oxford Univ. Press, 1953)
Morison, Elting, *Turmoil and Tradition: The Life and Times of Henry L. Stimson* (Boston: Houghton, 1960)
Perkins, Dexter, *Charles Evans Hughes and American Democratic Statesmanship* (Boston: Little-Brown, 1956)
Pogue, Forrest, *George C. Marshall: Ordeal and Hope, 1939–42* (New York: Viking, 1962)
Romanus, C. T., and Sunderland, Riley, *Stilwell's Mission to China* (Washington: Government Printing Office, 1952)
Rovere, Richard, and Schlesinger, Arthur, Jr., *The MacArthur Controversy and American Foreign Policy* (New York: Farrar, 1965)
Seabury, Paul, *Rise and Decline of the Cold War* (New York: Basic Books, 1967)
Spanier, John, *The Truman-MacArthur Controversy and the Korean War* (Cambridge: Harvard Univ. Press, 1959)

Snell, John L., *Illusion and Necessity: The Diplomacy of Global War, 1939–1945* (Boston: Houghton-Miffin, 1963)

Snell, John L. (ed.), *The Meaning of Yalta* (Baton Rouge: Louisiana State Univ. Press, 1956)

White, Theodore, *Fire in the Ashes* (New York: Sloan, 1953)

Wohlstetter, Barbara, *Pearl Harbor: Warning and Decision* (Palo Alto: Stanford Univ. Press, 1962)